D0611760

STREET SPANISH 2
The Best of Spanish Idioms

David Burke

John Wiley & Sons, Inc.
New York • Chichester • Weinheim • Brisbane • Singapore • Toronto

Once again, I'm forever grateful to Alfonso Moreno-Santa for his extraordinary contribution to this book. His organization, eye for detail, creative flair, and insight into the spoken Spanish language were essential in the creation of this book. He will always have my deepest appreciation and regard.

To say that Ty Semaka's illustrations are brilliant, hilarious, amazing, and magical would be an understatement. I consider myself so lucky to have found such talent all wrapped up in one person.

My special thanks and most sincere admiration go to Chris Jackson, my editor at John Wiley & Sons. To date, I don't believe there has been a word or an idiom created which describes someone who is as professional, reassuring, attentive, enthusiastic, motivated, and fun as Chris. He made the entire process truly enjoyable.

I must give an enormous thanks to Diane Aronson who is nothing less than amazing. It was an absolute pleasure to work with someone as masterful, thorough, adept, and affable as Diane.

Design and Production: David Burke
Copy Editor: Alfonso Moreno-Santa
Front Cover Illustration: Ty Semaka
Inside Illustrations: Ty Semaka

This book is printed on acid-free paper. ∞

Copyright © 1998 by David Burke. All rights reserved.
Published by John Wiley & Sons, Inc.
Published simultaneously in Canada.

No part of this publication may be reproduced, stored in a retrieval system or transmitted in any form or by any means, electronic, mechanical, photocopying, recording, scanning or otherwise, except as permitted under Sections 107 or 108 of the 1976 United States Copyright Act, without either the prior written permission of the Publisher, or authorization through payment of the appropriate per-copy fee to the Copyright Clearance Center, 222 Rosewood Drive, Danvers, MA 01923, (978) 750-8400, fax (978) 750-4744. Requests to the Publisher for permission should be addressed to the Permissions Department, John Wiley & Sons, Inc., 605 Third Avenue, New York, NY 10158-0012, (212) 850-6011, fax (212) 850-6008, E-Mail: PERMREQ@WILEY.COM.

This publication is designed to provide accurate and authoritative information in regard to the subject matter covered. It is sold with the understanding that the publisher is not engaged in rendering professional services. If professional advice or other expert assistance is required, the services of a competent professional person should be sought.

ISBN: 0-471-17971-X

Printed in the United States of America
10 9 8 7 6 5 4 3

CONTENTS

INTRODUCTION

To the outsider, idioms seem like a confusing secret code reserved only for the native speaker of Spanish. Idioms are certainly tricky beasts, because it is the *sum* of all the words in the phrase that must be interpreted, not each word by itself. In other words, the listener must never confuse the literal translation of an idiom with the underlying meaning of what is really being expressed or symbolized. In English, if you are told *"Get me a pizza... and step on it!"* you are not being instructed to go trample on a round piece of cheesy bread. You are simply being told to hurry, since *"step on it"* refers to "pressing down on" the accelerator of a car. The same applies to Spanish. For example, the popular idiom *"tomar el pelo a alguien"* literally "to take someone's hair," has nothing to do with hairpieces or haircuts. It simply means "to pull someone's leg."

In short, idioms are simply an imaginative and expressive way to communicate an idea or thought. In order to be considered truly proficient in Spanish, idioms must be learned, since they are consistently used in books, magazines, television, movies, songs, business, Spanish-speaking homes, and simply in everyday life.

For the nonnative speaker, learning **STREET SPANISH 2** will equal years of living in a Spanish-speaking country and reduce the usual time it takes to absorb the intricacies of slang and colloquialisms.

STREET SPANISH 2 is an entertaining guide made up of ten chapters, each divided into four primary parts:

- **DIALOGUE**

    Twenty to thirty popular Spanish idioms are presented as they may be heard in an actual conversation. A translation of the dialogue in standard English is always given on the opposite page, followed by a literal translation of the dialogue, often highlighting the idioms' eccentricities.

- **VOCABULARY**

    This section spotlights all of the idioms that were used in the dialogue and offers:

    1. An example of usage for each entry.

    2. An English translation of the dialogue.

    3. In addition, synonyms, antonyms, variations, or special notes are offered to give you a complete sense of the word or expression:

- ### PRACTICE THE VOCABULARY

  These word games include all of the idioms previously learned and will help you test yourself on your comprehension. *(The pages providing the answers to all the drills are indicated at the beginning of this section.)*

- ### DICTATION (Test your oral comprehension)

  Using an optional audio cassette *(see coupon on back page)*, the student will hear a paragraph containing many of the idioms from the opening dialogue. The paragraph will be read *as it would actually be heard* in a conversation, using frequent contractions and reductions.

- ### REVIEW

  Following each sequence of five chapters is a summary review encompassing all the words and expressions learned up to that point.

The secret to learning **STREET SPANISH 2** is by following this simple checklist:

- Make sure that you have a good grasp on each section before proceeding to the drills. If you've made more than two errors in a particular drill, simply go back and review...then try again! *Remember:* This is a self-paced book, so take your time. You're not fighting the clock!

- It's very important that you feel comfortable with each chapter before proceeding to the next. Words learned along the way may crop up in the following dialogues. So feel comfortable before moving on!

- Make sure that you read the dialogues and drills aloud. This is an excellent way to become comfortable speaking colloquially and begin thinking like a native.

If you have always prided yourself on being fluent in Spanish, you will undoubtedly be surprised and amused to encounter a whole new world of phrases usually hidden away in the Spanish language and usually reserved only for the native speaker...*until now!*

Legend

adjective

amuermado/a (estar) *adj.*
to be out of it, dazed.
SYNONYM: **aturdido** *adj.*

boldface words in parentheses are used before the main entry — they appear after the main entry for alphabetization purposes only, i.e. *estar amuermado/a.*

a term or expression equivalent in meaning to the main entry in boldface

buitre *m.* • **1.** cheapskate
• **2.** opportunist
• (lit.): vulture.

literal translation

chambear *v.* to work.
NOTE: **chamba** *f.* job.

useful information about the preceding entry

verb

de gala (estar) *exp.* to be all dressed up, to be in formal attire • (lit.): to be in full regalia.
VARIATION: **vestirse de gala** *exp.*
• (lit.): to dress oneself in full regalia.

feminine noun

a common variation of the main entry in boldface

expression

additional information about one or more of the words in the main entry.

dos dedos de (estar a) *exp.* to be on the verge of • (lit.): to be two fingers from.
ALSO: **dedo** *m.* a little bit • (lit.): finger
• beber un dedo de vino; to drink a drop of wine.

bracketed words in the main entry are optional

echar espumarajos [por la boca] *exp.*
to be furious, to foam at the mouth with rage
• (lit.): to throw foam [from the mouth].

a term or expression opposite in meaning of the main entry in boldface

nena *f.* girl, young woman.
ANTONYM: **nene** *m.* boy, young man.

masculine noun

pez gordo *m.* important person, "big wig"
• (lit.): fat fish.

02/31/03 - 1/13/04

¡Me estás *tomando el pelo*!

(trans.): You're **pulling my leg**!
(lit.): You're **taking my hair**!

¡Me estás tomando el pelo!

Carmen: Bueno, te voy a **poner al corriente**. No quiero **correr el rumor**, pero **anda de boca en boca**.

Pilar: ¡No te **andes con rodeos** y dime lo que pasa! Soy **todo oídos**.

Carmen: Tina dejó a Mark porque él estaba viendo a otra mujer **a escondidas**.

Pilar: ¡Me **estás tomando el pelo**! ¡Me he **quedado muda**! ¡Yo pensaba que a Mark **se le caía la baba por** ella! Bueno, **a decir verdad**, no me sorprende. Su papá le hizo lo mismo a su mamá. **De tal palo tal astilla**. **A primera vista**, parecía que Mark **tenía madera** para ser un buen marido. Bueno, **el hábito no hace al monje**.

Carmen: Primero, ella se dio cuenta de que él **le había dado gato por liebre** porque el anillo de compromiso era falso. Después, él le dijo que iba a trabajar tarde por un rato para ganar un poco de dinero extra para su luna de miel. Al principio, ella **se tragó el anzuelo**. Pero a ella **le dio mala espina** cuando él empezó a llegar a casa a las dos de la mañana. Ella sabía que **aquí había gato encerrado**. En fin, a la noche siguiente, ella le siguió hasta el apartamento de una mujer y ¡**le agarró con las manos en la masa**! ¡Ella **puso el grito al cielo**! Y por si **fuera poco**, ¡la otra mujer debe tener 25 años menos que él! Ella tendrá 21 años **cuando más**.

Pilar: ¡Espero que le **puso como un trapo**! Yo puedo perdonar muchas cosas, pero esta vez **se pasó de la raya**. Si eso me pasara a mí, ¡yo lo dejaba **en menos que canta un gallo**!

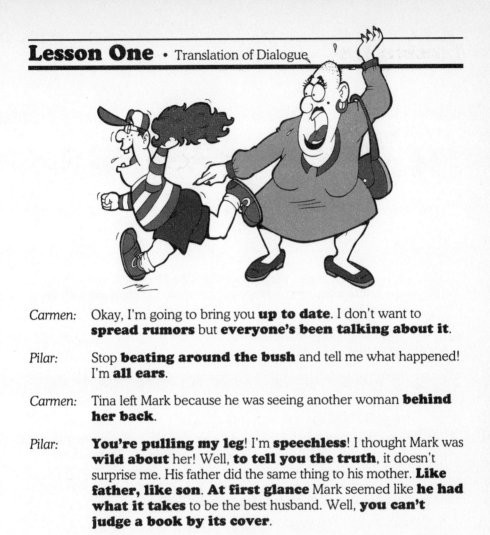

Carmen: Okay, I'm going to bring you **up to date**. I don't want to **spread rumors** but **everyone's been talking about it**.

Pilar: Stop **beating around the bush** and tell me what happened! I'm **all ears**.

Carmen: Tina left Mark because he was seeing another woman **behind her back**.

Pilar: **You're pulling my leg**! I'm **speechless**! I thought Mark was **wild about** her! Well, **to tell you the truth**, it doesn't surprise me. His father did the same thing to his mother. **Like father, like son**. **At first glance** Mark seemed like **he had what it takes** to be the best husband. Well, **you can't judge a book by its cover**.

Carmen: First, she realized that he **had pulled the wool over her eyes** because the engagement ring turned out to be a fake. Then he told her that he was going to work late in order to make extra money for their honeymoon. At first, she **bought it hook, line and sinker**. But he **aroused her suspicions** when he started coming home at two in the morning. She knew **there must be more here than meets the eye**. In short, the next night, she followed him to some woman's house and **caught him red-handed**! She **hit the ceiling**! **And as if that wasn't enough**, the other woman must be 25 years younger than he is! She must be 21 years old **at most**.

Pilar: I hope she **raked him over the coals**! I can forgive some things, but he really **went too far** this time. If something like that happened to me, I'd leave him **in a flash**!

3

You're taking my hair!

Carmen: Good, I'm going to **put you into the flow**. I don't want to **run the rumor** but **it's been walking from mouth to mouth**.

Pilar: Stop **walking with detours** and tell me what happened! I'm **all ears**.

Carmen: Tina left Mark because he was seeing another woman **on the hiding**.

Pilar: **You're taking my hair**! I'm **mute**! I thought Mark was **slobbering for** her! Well, **to say truth**, it doesn't surprise me. His father did the same thing to his mother. **From such stick comes such splinter**. **At first look** Mark seemed like **he had the wood** to be the best husband. Well, **the habit doesn't make the monk**.

Carmen: First, she realized that he **gave a cat instead of a hare** because the engagement ring turned out to be a fake. Then he told her that he was going to work late in order to make extra money for their honeymoon. At first, she **swallowed the hook**. But he **gave her a bad thorn** when he started coming home at two in the morning. She knew **there was a locked cat here**. In short, the next night, she followed him to some woman's house and **caught him with his hands in the dough**! She **put a scream in the sky**! **And as if that wasn't enough**, the other woman must be 25 years younger than he is! She must be 21 years old **when more**.

Pilar: I hope she **put him like a rag**! I can forgive some things, but he really **crossed the line** this time. If something like that happened to me, I'd leave him **in less time than a rooster can sing**!

Vocabulary

a escondidas *exp.* secretly, on the sly • (lit.): on the hiding [from the verb *esconder* meaning "to hide"].

> *example:*   Pablo y Sonia fueron al cine **a escondidas**.

> *translation:*   Pablo and Sonia went to the movies **secretly**.

> **ALSO:**   **a escondidas de** *exp.* without the knowledge of (lit.): on the hiding from.

a decir verdad *exp.* to tell you the truth • (lit.): to tell truth.

> *example:*   **A decir verdad**, te quiero mucho.

> *translation:*   **To tell you the truth**, I love you very much.

a primera vista *exp.* at first glance • (lit.): at first look.

> *example:*   **A primera vista**, Manolo parece buena persona.

> *translation:*   **At first glance**, Manolo seems like a nice guy.

> **ALSO -1:**   **con vistas a** *exp.* with a view to • (lit.): with views to.

> **ALSO -2:**   **estar a la vista** *exp.* to be in sight • (lit.): to be to the view.

> **ALSO -3:**   **hasta la vista** *exp.* see you later • (lit.): until the view [or next viewing of each other].

> **ALSO -4:**   **saltar a la vista** *exp.* to be obvious, to be self-evident • (lit.): to jump to view.

agarrar con las manos en la masa *exp.* to catch [someone] red-handed, to catch [someone] in the act • (lit.): to catch [someone] with the hands in the dough.

> *example:* A Luis lo **agarraron con las manos en la masa** cuando pretendía robar un carro.
>
> *translation:* Luis was **caught red-handed** when he was trying to steal a car.

> **SYNONYM -1:** **coger con las manos en la masa** *exp.* *(Spain)* • (lit.): to catch [someone] with his/her hands in the dough.

> **SYNONYM -2:** **coger/agarrar/atrapar en el acto** *exp.* • (lit.): to catch [someone] in the act.

> **SYNONYM -3:** **coger/agarrar/atrapar en plena acción** *exp.* • (lit.): to catch [someone] right in the action.

> **NOTE:** In these types of expressions, the verb *coger* is used primarily in Spain. In the rest of the Spanish-speaking world, *agarrar* and *atrapar* are most commonly used.

> **ALSO -1:** **caer en [las] manos de** *exp.* to fall into the hands of • (lit.): to fall into the hands of.

> **ALSO -2:** **cargar la mano** *exp.* to overcharge • (lit.): to load the hand.

> **ALSO -3:** **de mano en mano** *exp.* from hand to hand • (lit.): from hand in hand.

> **ALSO -4:** **írsele la mano** *exp.* to get carried away • (lit.): to let go the hand.

andar con rodeos *exp.* to beat around the bush • (lit.): to walk with detours.

> *example:* Alfredo siempre **anda con rodeos** cuando quiere explicar algún problema.
>
> *translation:* Alfredo always **beats around the bush** when he wants to explain a problem.

> **SYNONYM:** **andarse por las ramas** *exp.* • (lit.): to stroll/walk by the branches.

> **NOTE:** **emborrachar la perdiz** *exp.* *(Chile)* to beat around the bush • (lit.): to get the partridge drunk.

andar de boca en boca *exp.* to be generally known, to be in everyone's lips, to have everyone talking about it • (lit.): to walk from mouth to mouth.

> *example:* **Anda de boca en boca** que José se va a casar con Rocio.
>
> *translation:* **Everyone's talking about** José marrying Rocio.
>
> **SYNONYM -1:** **andar en boca de las gentes** *exp.* • (lit.): to walk on people's mouths.
>
> **SYNONYM -2:** **andar en boca de todos** *exp.* • (lit.): to walk in everyone's mouth.
>
> **ALSO -1:** **a pedir de boca** *exp.* smoothly • (lit.): to ask the mouth • *Todo salió a pedir de boca;* Everything went off smoothly.
>
> **ALSO -2:** **decir lo que se le viene a la boca** *exp.* to say whatever comes into one's mind • (lit.): to say what comes to one's mouth • *Javier dice lo que se le viene a la boca;* Javier says whatever comes to his mind.
>
> **ALSO -3:** **quedarse con la boca abierta** *exp.* to be flabbergasted • (lit.): to stay with one's mouth open.

caérsele la baba por *exp.* to be wild about, to love someone • (lit.): to slobber for.

> *example:* A Marcos **se le cae la baba por** Patricia.
>
> *translation:* Marcos **is wild about** Patricia.

correr el rumor *exp.* to be rumored • (lit.): to run the rumor.

> *example:* **Corre el rumor** que mañana van a despedir a Carlos.
>
> *translation:* **It's been rumored** that Carlos is going to get fired tomorrow.

cuando más *exp.* at most • (lit.): when more.

> *example:* Javier debe tener 18 años **cuando más**.
>
> *translation:* Javier must be 18 years old **at most**.

NOTE: This common expression is used primarily in Latin-American countries. • (lit.): when more.

ANTONYM: **cuando menos** *exp.* at least • (lit.): when less.

dar gato por liebre *exp.* to pull the wool over someone's eyes • (lit.): to give a cat instead of a hare.

example: **Le dieron gato por liebre** cuando Jorge compró esa casa. Tenía muchos problemas de plomería.

translation: They **pulled the wool over his eyes** when Jorge bought that house. It was full of plumbing problems.

ALSO: **correr como una liebre** *exp.* to run very fast, to run like a deer • (lit.): to run like a hare.

dar mala espina *exp.* to arouse one's suspicions • (lit.): to give a bad thorn.

example: A Mario **le dio mala espina** cuando vio a una persona salir del banco corriendo.

translation: It **aroused** Mario's **suspicions** when he saw a person running out of the bank.

de tal palo tal astilla *exp.* like father like son, a chip off the old block • (lit.): from such stick comes such splinter.

example: Alvaro quiere ser policía como su papá. **De tal palo tal astilla**.

translation: Alvaro wants to become a policeman like his dad. **Like father like son**.

el hábito no hace al monje *exp.* you can't judge a book by its cover • (lit.): the habit (attire) doesn't make the monk.

example: Alicia parece tan inocente pero en realidad es muy astuta. **El hábito no hace al monje**.

translation: Alicia looks very innocent but she's actually very sharp. **You can't judge a book by its cover**!

ALSO -1: **colgar los hábitos** *exp.* to leave the church • (lit.): to hang the habit (clothing wore by a member of a religious order).

ALSO -2: **tomar los hábitos** *exp.* to become a priest or a nun • (lit.): to take the habit.

en menos que canta un gallo *exp.* in a flash, as quick as a wink, in the winking of an eye • (lit.): in less time than a rooster can sing.

 example: David siempre termina su almuerzo **en menos que canta un gallo**.

 translation: David always finishes his lunch **in a flash**.

ALSO -1: **alzar/levantar uno el gallo** *exp.* to speak haughtily, to be arrogant • (lit.): to raise the rooster.

ALSO -2: **entre gallos y medianoche** *exp.* without warning, at an inconvenient time • (lit.): between roosters and midnight.

haber gato encerrado *exp.* there's more than meets the eye, there's something fishy • (lit.): there's a locked cat (here).

 example: Aquí **hay gato encerrado**. Esto no puede ser tan fácil.

 translation: **There's more here than meets the eye**. This can't be so easy.

pasarse de la raya *exp.* to go too far, to overstep one's bounds • (lit.): to cross the line.

 example: Yo creo que Jaime **se pasó de la raya** cuando intentó besar a Isabel.

 translation: I think Jaime **went a little too far** when he tried to kiss Isabel.

NOTE: This expression is so popular among Spanish-speakers, that often *de la raya* is omitted since it is already understood by the listener. For example: *Te has pasado;* You went too far.

ALSO: **tener a raya** *exp.* to keep in line • (lit.): to have in line.

poner a alguien como un trapo *exp.* to rake someone over the coals, to read someone the riot act • (lit.): to put someone like a rag.

example: Juan **puso al mesero como un trapo** porque no le trajo la comida a tiempo.

translation: Juan **raked the waiter over the coals** because he didn't bring him his meal on time.

ALSO: **tener lengua de trapo** *exp.* to speak incorrectly, to mumble • (lit.): to have a tongue made of rags.

poner al corriente *exp.* to bring up-to-date, to inform, to give the lowdown • (lit.): to put in the current or in the flow of knowledge.

example: Te voy a **poner al corriente** de lo que sucedió ayer en la oficina.

translation: I'm going to **bring you up-to-date** about what happened yesterday at the office.

SYNONYM: **poner al día** *exp.* • (lit.): to put to the day.

ALSO -1: **corriente** *f.* trend • *Las últimas corrientes de la moda;* the latest fashion trends.

ALSO -2: **llevarle/seguirle la corriente a uno** *exp.* to humor someone, • (lit.): to carry/to follow the current to someone.

poner el grito al cielo *exp.* to raise the roof, to scream with rage, to hit the ceiling • (lit.): to put a scream to the sky.

example: Lynda **puso el grito al cielo** cuando vio que la casa estaba muy sucia.

translation: Lynda **hit the ceiling** when she found out that the house was a real mess.

VARIATION: **poner en el grito al cielo** *exp.* • (lit.): to make a scandal.

> `SYNONYM -1:` **formar/armar un follón** *exp. (Spain)*. • (lit.): to make a scandal.
>
> `SYNONYM -2:` **hacer/formar un escándalo** *exp.* • (lit.): to make a scandal.
>
> `ALSO -1:` **a gritos** *exp.* at the top of one's voice • (lit.): shouting.
>
> `ALSO -2:` **dar gritos** *exp.* to shout • (lit.): to give shouts.

quedarse mudo/a *exp.* to be speechless, not to be able to respond, to be flabbergasted • (lit.): to remain mute.

> *example:* Antonio **se quedó mudo** cuando vio a Luisa en ese vestido anaranjado.
>
> *translation:* Antonio **was flabbergasted** when he saw Luisa wearing that orange dress.
>
> `SYNONYM -1:` **dejar sin habla** *exp.* • (lit.): to leave [someone] without speech.
>
> `SYNONYM -2:` **perder el habla** *exp.* • (lit.): to lose the speech.
>
> `ALSO:` **hacer hablar a los mudos** *exp.* to be capable of doing anything • (lit.): to make mute people talk.

tener madera para *exp.* to have what it takes, to be cut out for [something] • (lit.): to have the wood for [something].

> *example:* Augusto no **tiene madera para** ser bombero.
>
> *translation:* Augusto doesn't **have what it takes** to be a firefighter.
>
> `SYNONYM:` **estar hecho/a para** *exp.* • (lit.): to be made for.
>
> `ALSO:` **tocar madera** *exp.* to knock on wood • (lit.): to touch wood.

todo oídos (ser) *exp.* to be all ears • (lit.): to be all ears.

> *example:* Dime lo que pasó. **Soy todo oídos.**
>
> *translation:* Tell me what happened. **I'm all ears.**
>
> `ALSO -1:` **decir al oído** *exp.* to whisper in one's ear • (lit.): to tell [something] to the ear.
>
> `ALSO -2:` **entrar por un oído y salir por el otro** *exp.* to go in one ear and out the other • (lit.): to enter in one ear and exit the other.

ALSO -3:　**tener buen oído** *exp.* to have a good ear (for music) • (lit.): to have a good ear.

ALSO -4:　**tocar de oído** *exp.* to play (a musical instrument) by ear • (lit.): to touch by ear.

tomar el pelo a alguien *exp.* to pull someone's leg • (lit.): to take someone's hair.

example:　Creo que me estás **tomando el pelo**.

translation:　I think you're **pulling my leg**.

SYNONYM:　**hacerle guaje a uno** *exp. (Mexico)* • (lit.): to make a fool of someone.

ALSO -1:　**no tener un pelo de tonto** *exp.* to be nobody's fool • (lit.): not to even have one hair of stupid.

ALSO -2:　**no tener pelos en la lengua** *exp.* not to mince words • (lit.): not to have hairs in the tongue.

ALSO -3:　**ponerse los pelos de punta** *exp.* to have one's hair stand on end • (lit.): to put one's hair on end.

ALSO -4:　**por los pelos** *exp.* by the skin of one's teeth • (lit.): by the hairs.

ALSO -5:　**traído por los pelos** *exp.* far-fetched • (lit.): to be brought by the hairs.

tragar el anzuelo *exp.* to swallow it hook, line, and sinker • (lit.): to swallow the hook.

example:　Alberto **se tragó el anzuelo**. No sabe que lo que le dije es mentira.

translation:　Alberto **swallowed it hook, line, and sinker**. He doesn't know what I told him is a lie.

y por si fuera poco *exp.* and if that wasn't enough, and to top it off • (lit.): and if that wasn't enough.

example:　Hoy me robaron la cartera, **y por si fuera poco**, tenía mi cheque en ella.

translation:　Today my wallet was stolen, **and to top it off**, I had my paycheck in it.

Practice the Vocabulary

(Answers to Lesson One, p. 191)

A. Underline the appropriate word(s) that best complete(s) the phrase.

1. Álvaro (**ponme al corriente, dame corriente, llevame a la corriente**) de la situación; hace mucho tiempo que no sé nada.

2. Por la compañía (**salta la rana, corre el rumor, corre**) de que van a despedir a más de 100 empleados.

3. ¡Venga, cuéntame! (**Tengo un oído, Soy todo oídos, Oigo bien**).

4. El hotel parecía fantástico (**a vista de pájaro, a primera vista, primera pista**), pero en realidad no era tan bueno.

5. Augusto es muy bueno con las matemáticas; me recuerda a su padre. ¡Claro! (**de tal palo tal astilla, de una astilla del palo, es parecido**).

6. A María (**boicotea, se le cae la baba por, su bebé babea**) su hijo.

7. Cuando Alejandro se enfada, pierde el control y (**lava los trapos siempre, pone los trapos a remojar, pone a todo el mundo como un trapo**).

8. ¡(**Aquí hay un perro guardado, Aquí hay gato encerrado, El gato se ha escapado**)! Ayer Juan estaba muy triste y hoy está contentísimo.

9. Hay que hacerle (**tomar un trago, tragar el anzuelo, ir a pescar**) para que vaya a la fiesta sorpresa.

10. Este niño (**gusta la madera, es de madera, tiene madera de**) músico; a los cinco años ya tocaba el piano.

11. En cuanto se enteró de la noticia, Manuel llegó al hospital (**muy tarde, en menos que canta un gallo, me encantan los gallos**).

12. Cuando se dio cuenta de lo que le iba a costar, (**se puso muy tranquila, se fue al cielo, puso el grito en el cielo**).

B. Complete the following phrases by choosing the appropriate word(s) from the list below.

a escondidas	**dado gato por liebre**
se quedó mudo	**agarró / con las manos**
me tomes el pelo	**en la masa**
da mala espina	**anda de boca en boca**
se pasó de la raya	**puso al corriente**
anda con rodeos	**a primera vista**
	se le cae la baba

1. Esa casa me _____, entra y sale gente constantemente.

2. Tina pidió el divorcio cuando se enteró de que su marido veía a otra mujer _____.

3. Creo que Miguel _____; nunca debió pedirte dinero prestado.

4. Cuando Alfredo se enteró de la noticia, _____ .

5. A todos _____ por Pablito. ¡Es un cielo!

6. El detective _____ de todo a la policía.

7. Al año de comprar la casa, me di cuenta de que me habían _____, pues empezaron a salir problemas.

8. Álvaro siempre _____ cuando tiene que contarnos sus problemas.

9. El rumor ya _____; lo sabe todo el mundo.

10. ¡No _____! ¡Eso es imposible!

11. La policía _____ al ladrón _____.

12. Juan se enamoró _____.

C. Match the English phrase in the left column with the Spanish translation from the right. Mark the appropriate letter in the box.

1. She caught him red-handed.

2. I think that Jaime went too far.

3. She baked the cake in a flash.

4. At first glance it seems like there's no problem.

5. I'm speechless from his reaction.

6. The fact that he denied everything aroused my curiosity.

7. Stop beating around the bush!

8. Jose Luis is wild about Sara.

9. The children like to pull his leg.

10. I don't want to spread rumors.

11. They planned the party behind his father's back.

12. Ignacio has what it takes to be a matador.

A. No quiero **correr el rumor**.

B. Hizo el pastel **en menos que canta un gallo**.

C. Creo que Jaime **se pasó de la raya**.

D. Le **agarró con las manos en la masa**.

E. Le **dio mala espina** que negara todo.

F. Me he **quedado mudo** con su reacción.

G. ¡No **te andes con rodeos**!

H. A José Luis **se le cae la baba por** Sara.

I. Ignacio **tiene madera de** torero.

J. Planearon la fiesta **a escondidas de** su padre.

K. **A primera vista** no parece haber problema alguno.

L. A los niños les gusta **tomar el pelo**.

D. CROSSWORD
Fill in the crossword puzzle on page 18 by choosing the correct word(s) from the list below.

anzuelo	cuando	masa
astilla	escondidas	monje
baba	espina	mudo
boca	gallo	pelo
cielo	gato	raya
correr	liebre	rodeos
corriente	madera	trapo

ACROSS

1. **el hábito no hace al** _____ *exp.* you can't judge a book by its cover • (lit.): the habit (attire) doesn't make the monk.

15. **caérsele la** _____ **por** *exp.* to be wild about, to love someone • (lit.): to slobber for.

16. **dar** _____ **por liebre** *exp.* to pull the wool over the eyes, to deceive • (lit.): to give a cat instead of a hare

25. _____ **más** *exp.* at most • (lit.): when more.

29. **tomar el** _____ **a alguien** *exp.* to pull someone's leg • (lit.): to take someone's hair.

30. **pasarse de la** _____ *exp.* to go too far, to overstep one's bounds • (lit.): to cross the line.

39. **andar con** _____ *exp.* to beat around the bush • (lit.): to walk with detours.

40. **poner a alguien como un** _____ *exp.* to rake someone over the coals • (lit.): to put someone like a rag.

52. **a** _____ *exp.* secretly, on the sly.

DOWN

1. **agarrar con las manos en la** _____ *exp.* to catch [someone] red-handed, to catch [someone] in the act • (lit.): to catch [someone] with the hands in the dough.

7. **quedarse** _____ *exp.* to be speechless, not to be able to respond, to be flabbergasted.

13. **tener** _____ **para** *exp.* to have what it takes, to be cut out for • (lit.): to have the wood for [something].

16. **en menos que canta un** _____ *exp.* in a flash, as quick as a wink, in the blink of an eye • (lit.): in less time than a rooster can sing.

20. **poner el grito al** _____ *exp.* to raise the roof, to scream with rage, to hit the ceiling, to raise a big howl • (lit.): to put a scream to the sky.

24. **dar gato por** _____ *exp.* to pull the wool over the eyes, to deceive, to put something over • (lit.): to give a cat instead of a hare.

25. _____ **el rumor** *exp.* to be rumored • (lit.): to run the rumor.

36. **poner al** _____ *exp.* to bring up-to-date, to inform, to give the lowdown • (lit.): to put in the current or in the flow of knowledge.

37. **de tal palo tal** _____ *exp.* like father like son, a chip off the old block • (lit.): from such stick comes such splinter.

41. **tragar el** _____ *exp.* to swallow it hook, line, and sinker • (lit.): to swallow the hook.

47. **dar mala** _____ *exp.* to arouse one's suspicions • (lit.): to give a bad thorn.

50. **andar de** _____ **en boca** *exp.* to be generally known, to be in everyone's lips, to have eveyone talking about it • (lit.): to walk from mouth to mouth.

CROSSWORD PUZZLE

E. DICTATION
Test Your Aural Comprehension

(This dictation can be found in the Appendix on page 209.)

If you are following along with your cassette, you will now hear a series of sentences from the opening dialogue. These sentences will be read by a native speaker at normal conversational speed (which may seem fast to you at first). In addition, the words will be pronounced as you would actually hear them in a conversation, often including some common reductions.

The first time the sentences are presented, simply listen in order to get accustomed to the speed and heavy use of reductions. The sentences will then be read again with a pause after each to give you time to write down what you heard. The third time the sentences are read, follow along with what you have written.

1-14-04 -

¡La comida está *para chuparse los dedos!*

(trans.): The food is **delicious**!
(lit.): The food is **to suck one's fingers**!

¡La comida está para chuparse los dedos!

Ana: ¡Qué fiesta más divertida! La comida parece **para chuparse los dedos**. ¡Se me está **haciendo agua la boca**! ¡Vamos a comer!

Elena: ¡Un momento! Mira quien está **haciendo acto de presencia**. ¿Cómo se llama? **Lo tengo en la punta de la lengua**.

Ana: Se llama María Gómez. ¡Mira qué vestido tan pequeño y tan feo lleva puesto! Se está **poniendo en ridículo** ella misma. ¡Ese vestido **estuvo de moda** hace veinte años! Bueno, la verdad es que está **llamando la atención** pero **sobre gustos no hay nada escrito**. Yo le voy a **llevar la corriente**.

Elena: ¡Tengo una idea! Vamos a **darle esquinazo** o de lo contrario va a **hablar hasta por los codos** por horas. Tú ya sabes que es **muy ligera de palabra**. Siempre está preocupada por algo que casi siempre es **mucho ruido y pocas nueces** y siempre **habla como loca**.

Ana: **Tiene fama** de **ahogarse en un vaso de agua**. ¡Algunas veces **no entiendo ni papa** porque **habla a mil por hora**! La verdad es que **no la puedo ver ni en pintura**, porque dicen **las malas lenguas** que todas sus historias son **traídas por los pelos**. Entre tú y yo, creo que le **falta un tornillo**.

Ana: What a great party! The food looks **delicious**. It's **making my mouth water**! Let's go eat!

Elena: Wait! Look who **showed up**. Oh, what's her name? It's **on the tip of my tongue**.

Ana: Her name is Maria Gomez. Look at that horrible tiny dress she's wearing! It **makes her look ridiculous**. That hasn't been **in style** for twenty years! Well, she certainly is **attracting attention** but **to each his own**. I'm just going to **humor her**.

Elena: I have a better idea! Let's **avoid her** or she'll **talk our ears off** for hours. You know what a **blabbermouth** she is. She's always upset about something which is usually **a big deal about nothing** and she just **goes on and on**.

Ana: She **has a reputation** for **making a mountain out of a molehill**. Sometimes I **don't understand a thing** because she **talks too fast**! Frankly, I **can't stand her** because according to **gossip**, all her stories are so **far-fetched**. Just between you and me, I **don't think she's playing with a full deck**.

The food is to suck one's fingers!

Ana: What a great party! The food looks **to suck one's fingers**. It's **making my mouth water**! Let's go eat!

Elena: Wait! Look who's **making an act of presence**. Oh, what's her name? It's **on the tip of the tongue**.

Ana: She calls herself Maria Gomez. Look at that horrible tiny dress she's wearing! It **puts her in ridiculous**. That dress was **in style** twenty years ago! Well, she certainly is **calling for attention** but **on tastes, there is nothing written**. I'm just going **to carry the current to her**.

Elena: I have a better idea! Let's **give her a corner** or she'll **talk even with the elbows** for hours. You know **how light she is with words**. She's always upset about something which is usually **a lot of noise and very few walnuts** and she just **talks like a crazy person**.

Ana: She's **famous** for **drowning in a glass of water**. Sometimes I **don't understand a potato** because she **talks at a thousand kilometers per hour**! **To say truth**, I **can't even look at a painting of her** because according to **the bad tongues**, all her stories are so **carried by the hairs**. Just between you and me, I **think she's missing a screw**.

Vocabulary

ahogarse en un vaso de agua *exp.* to get all worked up about something, to make a mountain out of a molehill • (lit.): to drown in a glass of water.

> *example:* Antonio se preocupa demasiado de todo. Siempre **se ahoga en un vaso de agua**.
>
> *translation:* Antonio worries too much about everything. He always **makes a mountain out of a molehill**.
>
> **SYNONYM:** **ahogarse en poca agua** *exp.* • (lit.): to drown (oneself) in little water.
>
> **ALSO -1:** **ahogar el germen** *exp.* to nip in the bud • (lit.): to drown the germ.
>
> **ALSO -2:** **ahogar las penas** *exp.* to get drunk • (lit.): to drown the sorrow.

dar esquinazo *exp.* to avoid [someone], to ditch someone • (lit.): to give [someone] a corner.

> *example:* ¡Vamos a **darle esquinazo** a Julio! Es un pesado.
>
> *translation:* Let's **ditch** Julio! He's so annoying.
>
> **ALSO:** **doblar la esquina** *exp.* to turn the corner • (lit.): [same].

de moda (estar) *exp.* to be fashionable, to be chic, to be in style • (lit.): to be of fashion.

> *example:* Verónica siempre **se viste de moda**.
>
> *translation:* Verónica always **dresses in style**.
>
> **SYNONYM:** **de buen tono** *exp.* • (lit.): of good tone.
>
> **VARIATION:** **a la moda (estar)** *exp.* • (lit.): of good tone.
>
> **ALSO:** **ponerse de moda** *exp.* to come into style, to become fashionable • (lit.): to put into style.

faltar un tornillo *exp.* to have a screw lose • (lit.): to miss a screw.

> *example:* Yo creo que a Paco le **falta un tornillo**.
>
> *translation:* I think Paco **has a screw lose**.

SYNONYM -1: **estar chiflado/a** *exp.* • (lit.): to be crazy.

SYNONYM -2: **estar como una cabra** *exp.* • (lit.): to be like a goat.

SYNONYM -3: **estar tocado/a de la cabeza** *exp. (Spain)* • (lit.): to be touched in the head.

SYNONYM -4: **estar un poco loco/a** *exp.* • (lit.): to be a little bit crazy.

SYNONYM -5: **estar un poco sacado/a de onda** *exp. (Mexico)* • (lit.): to be a little taken from a wave.

SYNONYM -6: **tener flojos los tornillos** *exp.* • (lit.): to have loose screws.

SYNONYM -7: **tener los alambres pelados** *exp. (Chile)* • (lit.): to have peeled cables.

SYNONYM -8: **tener los cables cruzados** *exp. (Mexico)* • (lit.): to have crossed cables.

hablar [hasta] por los codos *exp.* to speak nonstop • (lit.): to talk even with the elbows.

> *example:* Pablo siempre **habla hasta por los codos** cuando viene a mi casa.
>
> *translation:* Pablo always **talks nonstop** when he comes to my house.

SYNONYM -1: **hablar como loco/a** *exp.* • (lit.): to speak like a crazy person.

SYNONYM -2: **hablar como una cotorra** *exp.* • (lit.): to talk like a parrot.

SYNONYM -3: **no parar la boca** *exp. (Mexico).* • (lit.): not to let the mouth stop.

SYNONYM -4: **ser de lengua larga** *exp.* • (lit.): to be of long tongue.

ALSO -1: **codo con codo** *exp.* close together, shoulder to shoulder • (lit.): elbow with elbow.

ALSO -2: **comerse los codos de hambre** *exp.* to be poverty-stricken • (lit.): to eat the elbows of hunger.

ALSO -3: **estar metido hasta los codos [en algo]** *exp.* to be up to one's neck [in something] • (lit.): to be in up to the elbows [in something].

hablar a mil por hora *exp.* to talk very fast, to talk a mile a minute • (lit.): to talk at one thousand kilometers per hour.

> *example:*   Lynda siempre **habla a mil por hora**.

> *translation:*   Lynda always **talks too fast**.

> **SYNONYM:**   **hablar a borbotones** *exp.* • (lit.): to talk like a torrent.

hablar como loco/a *exp.* to talk too much, to go on and on • (lit.): to talk like a crazy person.

> *example:*   Gabriela **habla como loca**. Nunca se calla.

> *translation:*   Gabriela **goes on and on**. She never shuts up.

> **SYNONYM -1:**   **hablar como un loro** *exp. (Spain)* • (lit.): to talk like a parrot.

> **SYNONYM -2:**   **hablar como una cotorra** *exp.* • (lit.): to talk like a parrot.

> **SYNONYM -3:**   **hablar hasta por las narices** *exp. (Spain)* • (lit.): to talk even through the nose.

> **SYNONYM -4:**   **hablar más que siete** *exp.* • (lit.): to talk more than seven (people).

> **SYNONYM -5:**   **hablar por los codos** *exp.* • (lit.): to talk through the elbows.

> **SYNONYM -6:**   **no parar la boca** *exp. (Mexico)* • (lit.): not to let the mouth stop.

> **ALSO -1:**   **hablar a tontas y a locas** *exp.* to say the first thing that comes into one's head • (lit.): to talk in a silly and crazy way.

> **ALSO -2:**   **hablar por hablar** *exp.* to talk for the sake of talking • (lit.): to talk just to talk.

> **ALSO -3:**   **ser mal hablado/a** *exp.* to be foul-mouthed • (lit.): to be bad spoken.

hacer acto de presencia *exp.* to put in an appearance, to show up • (lit.): to make an act of presence.

> *example:*   Jose Luis **hizo acto de presencia** en la fiesta de la escuela.

translation: Jose Luis **put in an appearance** at the school's party.

SYNONYM: **presentarse** *v.* • (lit.): to present oneself.

hacerse agua la boca *exp.* to make one's mouth water • (lit.): to make one's mouth water.

example: El olor de ese pan me está **haciendo agua la boca**.

translation: The smell of that bread is **making my mouth water**.

VARIATION: **hacerse la boca agua** *exp.*

las malas lenguas *exp.* gossip • (lit.): the bad tongues.

example: Dicen **las malas lenguas** que Darío va a dejar a Lucía por otra mujer.

translation: According to **gossip**, Dario is going to leave Lucia for another woman.

ALSO: **ser lengua larga** *exp.* to gossip • (lit.): to be of long tongue.

llamar la atención *exp.* to attract attention • (lit.): to call for attention.

example: Magda siempre **llama la atención** cuando se pone esa minifalda.

translation: Magda always **attracts attention** when she wears that mini-skirt.

ALSO: **prestar/poner atención** *exp.* to pay attention • (lit.): to borrow/to put attention.

llevar/seguir la corriente *exp.* to humor someone, to go along with • (lit.): to carry/follow the current to someone.

example: Me gusta **llevarle la corriente** a mi esposa porque no me gusta discutir con ella.

translation: I like **to humor** my wife because I don't like to argue with her.

ALSO -1: **corriente** *adj.* • **1.** common, ordinary • **2.** cheap / *una mujer corriente*; a cheap woman.

NOTE: This comes from the verb *correr* meaning "to run." Therefore, *una corriente* could be loosely translated as "a woman who runs around with more than one man."

ALSO -2: **dejarse llevar por la corriente** *exp.* to follow the crowd • (lit.): to let (oneself) be taken by the current.

mucho ruido y pocas nueces *exp.* much ado about nothing, a big fuss about nothing • (lit.): a lot of noise and very few walnuts.

example: Antonio tuvo una emergencia y me pidió que viniera enseguida. Pero en realidad era **mucho ruido y pocas nueces**.

translation: Antonio had an emergency and asked me to come over immediately. But it was really **a big fuss about nothing**.

muy ligero/a de palabra (ser) *exp.* to be a blabbermouth • (lit.): to be very light in words.

example: Rafael es **muy ligero de palabra**. Le gusta hablar demasiado.

translation: Rafael is a **blabbermouth**. He likes to talk too much.

SYNONYM -1: **charlatán (ser un)** *adj.* • (lit.): to be a charlatan.

SYNONYM -2: **chismoso (ser un)** *adj.* • (lit.): to be a gossip.

SYNONYM -3: **cuentista (ser un)** *adj.* • (lit.): to be a story teller.

ALSO -1: **a palabras necias, oídos sordos** *exp.* I'm going to let that go in one ear and out the other • (lit.): to foolish words, deaf ears.

ALSO -2: **sin cruzar la palabra** *exp.* not to say a word to each other • (lit.): without crossing a word.

ALSO -3: **tomarle la palabra** *exp.* to take one at one's word • (lit.): to take (someone's) word.

no entender ni papa *exp.* not to understand a thing • (lit.): not to understand a potato.

example: Cuando voy a clase de matemáticas, **no entiendo ni papa**.

    translation: When I go to my math class, **I don't understand a thing**.

    ALSO: **no saber ni papa de** *exp.* not to know a thing about, not to have a clue about.

no poder ver a alguien ni en pintura *exp.* not to be able to stand someone • (lit.): not to be able to look at a painting of someone (as the mere image would be too much to bear).

    example: No puedo **ver a Gonzalo ni en pintura**.

    translation: I **can't stand the site of Gonzalo**.

    SYNONYM -1: **no poder con** *exp.* • (lit.): not to be able to handle [something/someone].

    SYNONYM -2: **no tragar a alguien** *exp.* • (lit.): not to swallow someone.

    ALSO: **no ser un hueso fácil de roer** *exp.* not to be easy to tolerate • (lit.): not to be an easy bone to gnaw.

para chuparse los dedos *exp.* said of something delicious • (lit.): to suck or lick one's fingers.

    example: Esta comida está **para chuparse los dedos**.

    translation: This food is **delicious**.

    NOTE: A popular Spanish advertisement goes as follows: *Kentucky Fried Chicken está para chuparse los dedos;* Kentucky Fried Chicken is finger lickin' good.

    SYNONYM: **estar a toda madre** *exp. (Mexico)* • This popular Mexican expression is used to express enthusiasm about food as well as situations • (lit.): to be like an entire mother.

poner en ridículo *exp.* to make a fool out of someone • (lit.): to put [someone] in ridiculous.

    example: Jorge está **poniendo en ridículo** a su jefe a propósito.

    translation: Jorge is **making a fool out of** his boss on purpose.

    ALSO: **hacer el ridículo** *exp.* to make a fool of oneself • (lit.): to make the ridiculous.

sobre gustos no hay nada escrito *exp.* to each his own [taste] • (lit.): on tastes, there is nothing written (meaning: when it come to tastes, there are no rules).

> *example:* ¡Mira qué zapatos lleva Adolfo! **Sobre gustos no hay nada escrito**.
>
> *translation:* Look at the shoes Adolfo is wearing! **To each his own taste**.
>
> **SYNONYM:** **en gustos se rompen géneros** *exp.* • (lit.): in tastes one can break genders.
>
> **ALSO -1:** **de buen/mal gusto** *exp.* in good/bad taste • (lit.): [same].
>
> **ALSO -2:** **eso va en gustos** *exp.* that's a matter of taste • (lit.): that goes in tastes.

tener algo en la punta de la lengua *exp.* to have something on the tip of the tongue • (lit.): [same].

> *example:* No me acuerdo de cómo se llama ese tipo, pero lo **tengo en la punta de la lengua**.
>
> *translation:* I don't remember that guy's name but **it's on the tip of my tongue**.
>
> **ALSO -1:** **tener la lengua de víbora** *exp.* to have a poisonous tongue • (lit.): to have the tongue of a viper.
>
> **ALSO -2:** **tener la lengua larga** *exp.* to be a blabbermouth • (lit.): to have a long tongue.

tener fama de *exp.* to have a reputation for • (lit.): to have fame for.

> *example:* Ese restaurante **tiene fama de** servir buena comida.
>
> *translation:* That restaurant **has a reputation for** good food.
>
> **ALSO:** **tener mala/buena fama** *exp.* to have a bad/good reputation • (lit.): to have bad/good fame.

traer por los pelos *exp.* to be farfetched • (lit.): to be carried by the hairs.

> *example:* Me parece que su cuento es **traído por los pelos**.
>
> *translation:* I think his story is a little **farfetched**.

Practice the Vocabulary

(Answers to Lesson Two, p. 193)

A. Rewrite the following sentences by replacing the italicized word(s) in the left column with the slang translation from the right.

1. El pollo está *buenísimo*
    _____

2. A Alfonso *no le gustan* los mariscos.
    _____

3. *Hay gustos para todo.*
    _____

4. Ahora *se lleva* la minifalda.
    _____

5. Marta *habla muchísimo.*
    _____

6. Eva *estuvo* en la reunión.
    _____

7. Jesús *no comprende nada* de inglés.
    _____

8. David *está completamente loco.*
    _____

9. *Me encanta* pensar en las tortillas que hace Pepa.
    _____

10. Rafael *se preocupa demasiado por pequeños problemas.*
    _____

A. **habla por los codos**

B. **hizo acto de presencia**

C. **no puede ver algo/ alguien ni en pintura**

D. **le falta un tornillo**

E. **está de moda**

F. **no entiende ni papa**

G. **se ahoga en un vaso de agua**

H. **sobre gustos no hay nada escrito**

I. **para chuparse los dedos**

J. **se me hace agua la boca**

B. Complete the following phrases by choosing the appropriate word(s) from the list below. Make all necessary changes.

darle esquinazo

dicen las malas lenguas

en la punta de la lengua

entiendo ni papa

están de moda

habla como un loco

llama la atención

llevarle la corriente

muy ligera de palabra

para chuparse los dedos

pone en ridículo

tiene fama de

1. Déjame pensar, tengo el nombre _____.

2. _____ que Javier tiene problemas en casa.

3. Alfonso _____ ligón. ¡Es tan guapo!

4. Está un poco loco, así que es mejor _____.

5. Vicente es pesadísimo. Vamos a intentar _____.

6. No entiendo a Juan, _____.

7. Cada vez que habla, _____ a alguien.

8. No _____ de alemán.

9. Cristina no piensa las cosas, es _____.

10. Los años 60 (sesenta) _____ otra vez.

11. Estefanía es tan guapa, que _____ donde va.

12. Este año la comida del día de Acción de Gracias estaba

    _____.

C.   Underline the synonym.

1. **para chuparse los dedos**:
   a. buenísimo
   b. guapísimo

2. **faltar un tornillo**:
   a. estar desatornillado
   b. estar loco

3. **hacer acto de presencia**:
   a. presentador
   b. estar presente

4. **hablar a mil por hora**:
   a. hablar muy lento
   b. hablar muy rápido

5. **hablar por los codos**:
   a. hablar mucho
   b. hablar poco

6. **traer por los pelos**:
   a. ser inteligente
   b. ser poco probable

7. **ahogarse en un vaso de agua**:
   a. echarse agua por encima
   b. preocuparse por algo poco importante

8. **no entender ni papa**:
   a. no gustar las papas
   b. no entender nada

9. **sobre gustos no hay nada escrito**:
   a. hay gustos para todo
   b. no hay libros sobre gustos

10. **no poder ver a alguien ni en pintura**:
    a. no gustar alguien
    b. ser alérgico a la pintura

11. **mucho ruido y pocas nueces**:
    a. parecer más de lo que realmente es
    · b. haber más ruidos que nueces

12. **hacer[se] agua la boca**:
    a. gustar algo mucho
    b. tener mucha sed

D. Complete the dialogue using the list below.

falta un tornillo	**más ruido que nueces**
hace agua la boca	**no pudieras verlo ni**
hicieron acto de presencia	** en pintura**
las malas lenguas	**pone en ridículo**
ligero de palabra	**tengo en la punta de**
llamar la atención	** la lengua**
llevarle la corriente	**tengo fama**

Ana: El año pasado estuvimos comiendo en casa de Pepa. Aún se me

_____ pensando en lo que cocinó; todo estaba

buenísimo.

Elena: Sí, ya me contaron. Por cierto, ¿_____ los Rodríguez?

Ana: Sí, estuvieron allí con su hijo mayor ¿Cómo se llama?

Elena: Lo _____, pero no consigo acordarme.

Ana: Bueno, ya nos acordaremos.

Elena: De todas formas, él no es como su padre que _____ a

todo el mundo contando intimidades de cada uno.

Ana: Ya, su padre es un poco _____. Le gusta

_____. Creo que en definitiva, le _____.

Elena: Hablas de él como si _____.

Ana: Bueno, tampoco es para tanto. Sólo hay que _____ y al

final, es hasta gracioso.

Elena: No entiendo lo que dices. Por un lado no te gusta y por otro te

parece gracioso. ¡Vaya contradicción!

Ana: Ya, _____ de contradictorio, pero en realidad es

_____.

Elena: Bueno, Ana, tengo que irme, no vayan a decir _____

que me tomo unos descansos muy largos.

Ana: Hasta luego.

E. DICTATION
Test Your Aural Comprehension

(This dictation can be found in the Appendix on page 209.)

If you are following along with your cassette, you will now hear a series of sentences from the opening dialogue. These sentences will be read by a native speaker at normal conversational speed (which may seem fast to you at first). In addition, the words will be pronounced as you would actually hear them in a conversation, often including some common reductions.

The first time the sentences are presented, simply listen in order to get accustomed to the speed and heavy use of reductions. The sentences will then be read again with a pause after each to give you time to write down what you heard. The third time the sentences are read, follow along with what you have written.

2004-2-7 = 3week

Tengo que consultarlo con la almohada.

(trans.): I have **to sleep on it**.
(lit.): I have **to consult my pillow about it**.

Tengo que consultarlo con la almohada

Sergio: Marco y el jefe han estado **a puerta cerrada** varias horas. Me pregunto qué está pasando.

Ricardo: Bueno, esta mañana me dijo el jefe que después de **consultarlo con la almohada**, finalmente ha decidido **echar a la calle** a Marco, pero **del dicho al hecho hay mucho trecho**. Después de todo, no solo ha sido **su brazo derecho** por más de un año, sino que además **son uña y carne**.

Sergio: ¡Tienes razón! Marco es su mejor amigo. ¿Cual fue el problema?

Ricardo: **Está tan claro como el agua**. El Jefe estaba **echando chispas** porque Marco ha estado **echandose un trago** en horas de trabajo, y esto lo hace **sin falta**.

Sergio: He **perdido el habla**. Me alegro de no **estar en su pellejo**. A lo mejor el jefe cambia de opinión, porque Marco es tan buen trabajador. Siempre **suda la gota gorda** y todos lo saben.

Ricardo: Estás **gastando saliva en balde**. Una vez que el jefe toma una decisión, nunca **da su brazo a torcer**. Además, él ya ha hablado con Marco de este asunto otras veces, pero parece que **le entra por un oído y le sale por el otro**. Creo que el jefe ya está **hasta la coronilla** y por eso ha **cortado por lo sano**. Así que, **hoy por hoy**, **por las buenas o por las malas**, Marco va a tener que empezar a buscar otro trabajo.

Sergio: Marco and the boss have been **behind closed doors** for hours. I wonder what's going on.

Ricardo: Well, this morning the boss told me that after **sleeping on it**, he's finally decided **to fire** Marco which is **easier said than done**. After all, he's not only been his **right-hand man** for a year but they're also **close friends**.

Sergio: That's right! Marco is his best friend. What was the problem?

Ricardo: **It's as plain as the nose on your face**. The boss was **furious** because Marco has been **drinking** on the job everyday **without fail**.

Sergio: I'm **speechless**. I'm glad I'm not **in his shoes**. Maybe the boss would reconsider since Marco is such a good worker. He **works like a dog** here and everyone knows it.

Ricardo: You're **wasting your breath**. Once the boss makes a decision, he **sticks to his guns**. Besides, he's talked to Marco about this before but **it all seems to go in one ear and out the other**. I think the boss finally got **fed up** which is why he's **taking drastic measures**. So **as of right now**, **whether he likes it or not**, Marco is going to have to start looking for another job.

I have to consult my pillow about it

Sergio: Marco and the boss have been **at closed doors** for hours. I wonder what's going on.

Ricardo: Well, this morning the boss told me that after **consulting about it with his pillow**, he's finally decided **to throw Marco to the street** which is **from what someone says to the facts, there's a long way to go**. After all, he's not only been his **right arm** for a year but they're also **fingernail and flesh**.

Sergio: That's right! Marco is his best friend. What was the problem?

Ricardo: **It's as clear as water**. The boss was **throwing sparks** because Marco has been **throwing a swallow** during work everyday **without fail**.

Sergio: I've **lost my speech**. I'm glad I'm not **in his skin**. Maybe the boss would reconsider since Marco is such a good worker. He **sweats the fat drop here** and everyone knows it.

Ricardo: You're **wasting your saliva in vain**. Once the boss makes a decision, he **doesn't give his arm to be twisted**. Besides, he's talked to Marco about this before but **it all seems to go in one ear and out the other**. I think the boss finally got **up to the crown with him** which is why he's **cutting it off and leaving only the healthy part**. So **today by today, by the goods or by the bads**, Marco is going to have to start looking for another job.

Vocabulary

a puerta cerrada *exp.* behind closed doors • (lit.): at closed door.

> *example:* Los ejecutivos de la empresa tuvieron una reunión **a puerta cerrada**.

> *translation:* The company's executives had a meeting **behind closed doors**.

> **SYNONYM -1:** **en clausura** *exp.* • (lit.): in confinement (said of life in a monastery).

> **SYNONYM -2:** **en privado** *exp.* • (lit.): in private.

> **ANTONYM:** **a puerta abierta** *exp.* with opened doors • (lit.): at opened door.

> **ALSO -1:** **cerrar todas las puertas** *exp.* to close all avenues to someone • (lit.): to close all the doors.

> **ALSO -2:** **dar con la puerta en las narices** *exp.* to slam the door in someone's face • (lit.): to give the door in the nose.

consultarlo con la almohada *exp.* to sleep on eat • (lit.): to consult it with the pillow.

> *example:* Esa decisión tan importante, tendré que **consultarla con la almohada**.

> *translation:* It's such a big decision, I will have **to sleep on it**.

cortar por lo sano *exp.* to take drastic measures • (lit.): to cut (something off) and leave only the healthy parts.

> *example:* Voy a **cortar por los sano** y empezar de nuevo.

> *translation:* I'm going **to take drastic measures** and start all over again.

ALSO: **sano y salvo** *exp.* safe and sound • (lit.): healthy and saved.

del dicho al hecho hay mucho trecho *exp.* easier said than
done • (lit.): from what someone says to the facts, there's a long way to go.

>   *example:*   Tienes que despedir a Juan, pero **del dicho al hecho hay mucho trecho**. Es tu mejor amigo.

>   *translation:*   You have to fire Juan, but **it's easier said than done**. He's your best friend.

echar a alguien a la calle *exp.* to fire someone, to can someone •
(lit.): to throw someone to the street.

>   *example:*   Parece que a Tomás lo **echaron a la calle** porque siempre llegaba tarde al trabajo.

>   *translation:*   It looks like they **fired** Tomas because he was always late to work.

SYNONYM -1:   **arrojar a la calle** *exp.* • (lit.): to throw [someone/something] to the street.

SYNONYM -2:   **correr** *v. (Mexico).* • (lit.): to run.

SYNONYM -3:   **despedir** *v.* • (lit.): to say goodbye to.

echar chispas *exp.* to be furious, to be mad or angry • (lit.): to throw
sparks.

>   *example:*   El jefe estaba **echando chispas** cuando se enteró que Andrés llamó enfermo tres veces esta semana.

>   *translation:*   The boss **was furious** when he found out Andres called in sick for the third time this week.

SYNONYM -1:   **echar fuego por las orejas** *exp.* • (lit.): to throw fire through the ears.

echarse un trago *exp.* to have a drink • (lit.): to throw a swallow.

    example: A mi papá le gusta **echarse un trago** después del trabajo.

    translation: My father likes **to have a drink** after work.

    NOTE: The verb *tragar,* literally meaning "to swallow," is commonly used to mean "to eat voraciously." It is interesting to note that as a noun, *trago* means "a drink." However, when used as a verb, *tragar* takes on the meaning of "to eat" • *¿Quieres echar un trago?;* Would you care for a drink? • *¿Qué quieres tragar?;* What would you like to eat?

    SYNONYM -1: **echarse un fogonazo** *exp. (Mexico)* • (lit.): to throw oneself a flash.

    SYNONYM -2: **empinar el cacho** *exp. (Chile)* • (lit.): to raise the piece.

    SYNONYM -3: **empinar el codo** *exp.* • (lit.): to raise the elbow.

    SYNONYM -4: **pegarse un palo** *exp. (Cuba, Puerto Rico, Dominican Republic, Colombia)* • (lit.): to stick oneself a gulp.

    ALSO: **duro de tragar** *exp.* hard to believe • (lit.): hard to swallow.

el brazo derecho *exp.* right-hand man • (lit.): the right arm.

    example: Alfonso es **el brazo derecho** de Carlos.

    translation: Alfonso is Carlos's **right-hand man**.

    ALSO -1: **con los brazos abiertos** *exp.* with open arms.

    ALSO -2: **en los brazos de Morfeo (estar)** *exp.* to sleep • (lit.): in the arms of Morpheus (the god of sleep and dreams).

    ALSO -3: **no dar el brazo a torcer** *exp.* not to give in • (lit.): not to give the arm to be twisted.

    SEE: **no dar el brazo a torcer**, *p. 45.*

en el pellejo de alguien (estar) *exp.* to be in someone's shoes • (lit.): to be in someone's skin (hide).

　　example: No me gustaría **estar en su pellejo cuando le pida un aumento al jefe.**

　　translation: I wouldn't like **to be in his shoes** when he asks the boss for a raise.

　　SYNONYM: **en la piel de (estar)** *exp.* • (lit.): to be in one's skin.

　　ALSO -1: **arriesgarse el pellejo** *exp.* to risk one's neck • (lit.): to risk one's skin (or hide).

　　ALSO -2: **salvarse el pellejo** *exp.* to save one's skin • (lit.): to save one's skin (or hide).

entrar por un oído y salir por el otro *exp.* to go in one ear and out the other • (lit.): to go in one ear and out the other.

　　example: Todo lo que le digo a Isabel **le entra por un oído y le sale por el otro**.

　　translation: Anything that I tell Isabel **goes in one ear and out the other**.

　　SYNONYM: **hacer caso omiso de** *exp.* • (lit.): to take no notice of.

　　ALSO -1: **aguzar el oído** *exp.* to prick up one's ear • (lit.): to sharpen one's ear.

　　ALSO -2: **decir [algo] al oído** *exp.* to whisper [something] in one's ear • (lit.): to say [something] to the ear.

　　ALSO -3: **llegar a oídos de** *exp.* to reach the ears of • (lit.): to arrive to the ears of.

　　ALSO -4: **ser todo oídos** *exp.* to be all ears • (lit.): [same].

gastar saliva en balde *exp.* to waste one's breath [while explaining something to someone] • (lit.): to waste one's saliva in vain.

　　example: No me gusta **gastar saliva en balde**. Yo sé que de todas maneras no me entenderías.

　　translation: I don't like to **waste my breath**. I know you wouldn't understand me anyway.

　　ALSO: **de balde** *exp.* free of charge • (lit.): in vain.

hasta la coronilla de (estar) *exp.* to be fed up with, to be sick of [something or someone] • (lit.): to be up to the crown with.

>*example:* Estoy **hasta la coronilla de** Marcos.

>*translation:* I'm **fed up with** Marcos.

>**SYNONYM -1:** **estar harto de [alguien]** *exp.* • (lit.): to be fed up with [someone].

>**SYNONYM -2:** **estar hasta las cejas de** *exp.* • (lit.): to be up to the eyebrows.

>**ALSO -1:** **tener a uno entre ceja y ceja** *exp.* to be set on • (lit.): to have someone between eyebrow and eyebrow.

>**ALSO -2:** **tener entre cejas** *exp.* to take a dislike to • (lit.): to take someone between eyebrows.

hoy por hoy *exp.* as of right now • (lit.): today by today.

>*example:* **Hoy por hoy** no tengo dinero.

>*translation:* **As of right now**, I don't have money to pay you.

>**ALSO -1:** **de hoy en adelante** *exp.* from now on • (lit.): from today forward.

>**ALSO -2:** **hoy en día** *exp.* nowadays • (lit.): today in day.

>**ALSO -3:** **hoy mismo** *exp.* today, this very day • (lit.): today the same.

no dar el brazo a torcer *exp.* to stick to one's guns, not to give in, not to have one's arm twisted • (lit.): not to give one's arm to be twisted.

>*example:* Pablo **nunca da su brazo a torcer**. Es muy testarudo.

>*translation:* Pablo always **sticks to his guns**. He's very stubborn.

>**ANTONYM:** **dar el brazo a torcer** *exp.* to give in, to have one's arm twisted • (lit.): to give one's arm to be twisted.

perder el habla *exp.* to be speechless • (lit.): to lose one's speech.

> *example:* **Perdí el habla** cuando vi a María en ese vestido. ¡Era tan corto!

> *translation:* **I was speechless** when I saw Maria wearing that dress. It was so short!

> **SYNONYM:** **quedarse mudo/a** *exp.* • (lit.): to remain/become mute.

por las buenas o por las malas *exp.* whether one likes it or not, one way or another • (lit.): by the goods or by the bads.

> *example:* David va a ganar la carrera **por las buenas o por las malas**.

> *translation:* David is going to win the race **one way or another**.

> **VARIATION:** **a las buenas o a las malas** *exp.* • (lit.): to the good ones or to the bad ones.

> **SYNONYM:** **de una manera u otra** *exp.* • (lit.): one way or another.

sin falta *exp.* without fail • (lit.): without fail.

> *example:* Mañana voy a comprarme un abrigo nuevo **sin falta**.

> *translation:* Tomorrow I'm going to buy myself a new coat **without fail**.

> **ALSO -1:** **a falta de** *exp.* for lack of • (lit.): [same].

> **ALSO -2:** **hacer falta** *exp.* to need • (lit.): to make fail.

sudar la gota gorda *exp.* to sweat blood, to make a superhuman effort • (lit.): to sweat the fat drop.

> *example:* Cuando voy al gimnasio siempre **sudo la gota gorda**.

> *translation:* When I go to the gym, I always **sweat bullets**.

> **SYNONYM:** **sudar petróleo** *exp.* • (lit.): to sweat petroleum.

> **ALSO -1:** **no ver ni gota** *exp.* not to be able to see a thing • (lit.): not to even see a drop.

> **ALSO -2:** **sudar a chorros** *exp.* to sweat like a pig • (lit.): to sweat in spurs, gushes, streams, etc.

tan claro como el agua (estar) *exp.* it's as plain as the nose on one's face • (lit.): as clear as water.

    example: ¡Está **tan claro como el agua**! Guillermo odia su trabajo.

    translation: It's **as plain as day**! Guillermo hates his job.

> **SYNONYM:** **tan claro como que yo me llamo [fill in your own name]** *exp.* • (lit.): it's as clear as my name is [fill in your own name].

> **ALSO -1:** **agua pasada no mueve molino** *exp.* that's all water under the bridge • (lit.): passed water doesn't move a mill.

> **ALSO -2:** **nadar entre dos aguas** *exp.* to be on the fence • (lit.): to swim between two waters.

uña y carne (ser como) *exp.* to be inseparable, to be hand in glove, to be as thick as thieves • (lit.): to be fingernail and flesh.

    example: Oscar y Elena son **como uña y carne**.

    translation: Oscar and Elena are **inseparable**.

> **SYNONYM:** **como uña y mugre** *exp. (Mexico)* • (lit.): like a fingernail and its dirt.

> **ANTONYM:** **llevarse como perro y gato** *exp.* to fight like cats and dogs • (lit.): to get along like dog and cat.

> **SEE:** **llevarse como perro y gato**, *p. 103.*

> **ALSO -1:** **esconder las uñas** *exp.* to hide one's true intentions • (lit.): to hide the fingernails.

> **ALSO -2:** **sacar las uñas** *exp.* to show one's true colors • (lit.): to show the fingernails.

Practice the Vocabulary

(Answers to Lesson Three, p. 195)

A. Fill in the blank with the correct word(s) using the list below.

brazo derecho
consultarlo con la
   almohada
cortar por lo sano
dar su brazo a torcer
echaba chispas
hasta la coronilla de

hoy por hoy
hubiera estado en su pellejo
le entra por un oído y le sale
   por el otro
perdí el habla
por las buenas o por las malas
uña y carne

1. Aquí hay que _____; ésto no puede seguir igual.

2. Estoy _____ Manuel; cada vez que digo algo se enfada.

3. Jaime nunca escucha, todo _____.

4. Alfredo y Eva son _____; siempre están juntos.

5. Es una decisión muy importante; tengo que _____.

6. Nuestro jefe sólo confía en Pepe, es su _____.

7. _____ cuando me enteré de que Antonio había intentado salir con mi mujer.

8. _____ hay que hacerle entrar en razón.

9. _____, ella es lo mejor que me ha pasado en la vida.

10. Augusto estaba que _____ cuando supo que le iba a costar tanto dinero.

11. Raúl no quería _____, pero al final tuvo que reconocerlo.

12. Si yo _____, no hubiera aguantado ni la mitad de lo que él aguantó.

B. Match the English phrase in the left column with the Spanish translation from the right. Mark the appropriate letter in the box.

☐ 1. The meeting was held behind closed doors.

☐ 2. I think you should decide after sleeping on it.

☐ 3. Over a thousand workers are going to be fired.

☐ 4. It's easier said than done.

☐ 5. We sweat blood trying to move that piece of furniture.

☐ 6. As of today, Gordillo is the best soccer player in the world.

☐ 7. We drink once in a while.

☐ 8. Don't waste your breath. I won't believe you anyway.

☐ 9. It's as plain as day.

☐ 10. I'm fed up with him.

☐ 11. Eva and Alfredo are inseparable.

☐ 12. I'm so fat! I'm going to take drastic action. Starting today, I'm not going to eat any more sweets.

A. Van a **echar a la calle** a más de mil trabajadores.

B. La reunión se celebró **a puerta cerrada**.

C. ¡Estoy tan gordo! Voy a **cortar por lo sano**. A partir de hoy, no voy a comer más dulces.

D. Eva y Alfredo son **uña y carne**.

E. Nos **echamos un trago** de vez en cuando.

F. Estoy **hasta la coronilla de** él.

G. **Hoy por hoy**, Gordillo es el mejor futbolista del mundo.

H. No **gastes saliva en balde**; no te voy a creer de ninguna forma.

I. **Del dicho al hecho hay mucho trecho**.

J. Creo que debes decidirlo después de **consultarlo con la almohada**.

K. **Sudamos la gota gorda** intentando mover ese mueble.

L. **Está tan claro como el agua**.

C. CROSSWORD

Fill in the crossword puzzle on page 52 by choosing the correct word(s) from the list below.

agua	chispas	pellejo
almohada	coronilla	puerta
brazo	falta	saliva
buenas	gorda	sano
calle	habla	torcer
carne	otro	trago
		trecho

ACROSS

7. **del dicho al hecho hay mucho** _____ *exp.* easier said than done • (lit.): from what someone says to the facts, there's a long way to go.

17. **tan claro como el** _____ **(estar)** *exp.* it's as plain as the nose on one's face • (lit.): as clear as water.

22. **sudar la gota** _____ *exp.* to sweat blood, to make a superhuman effort • (lit.): to sweat the fat drop.

24. **a** _____ **cerrada** *exp.* behind closed doors • (lit.): at closed door.

30. **perder el** _____ *exp.* to be speechless • (lit.): to lose one's speech.

40. **hasta la** _____ **de (estar)** *exp.* to be fed up with, to be sick of [something or someone].

49. **cortar por lo** _____ *exp.* to take drastic measures • (lit.): to cut (something off) and leave only the healthy parts.

51. **entrar por un oído y salir por el** _____ *exp.* to go in one ear and out the other.

55. **echar a alguien a la _____** *exp.* to fire someone, to can someone • (lit.): to throw someone to the street.

56. **el _____ derecho** *exp.* right-hand man • (lit.): the right arm.

64. **uña y _____ (ser como)** *exp.* to be inseparable, to be hand in glove • (lit.): to be fingernail and flesh.

DOWN

7. **echarse un _____** *exp.* to have a drink • (lit.): to throw a swallow.

14. **sin _____** *exp.* without fail • (lit.): without fail.

20. **en el _____ de (estar)** *exp.* to be in someone's shoes • (lit.): to be in someone's skin (hide).

21. **por las _____ o por las malas** *exp.* whether one likes it or not, one way or another.

35. **gastar _____ en balde** *exp.* to waste one's breath [while explaining something to someone] • (lit.): to waste one's saliva in vain.

36. **no dar el brazo a _____** *exp.* to stick to one's guns, not to give in, not to have one's arm twisted • (lit.): not to give one's arm to be twisted.

40. **echar _____** *exp.* to be furious, to be mad or angry • (lit.): to throw sparks.

41. **consultarlo con la _____** *exp.* to sleep on eat • (lit.): to consult it with the pillow.

CROSSWORD PUZZLE

D. Underline the appropriate word(s) that best complete(s) the phrase.

1. Debes ir (**sin falta**, **con falta**, **interesante**) a ver esa película.

2. Estoy que (**chispas**, **echo chismes**, **echo chispas**) después de enterarme que fueron los niños quienes rompieron el jarrón.

3. Vamos a (**echarnos un trago**, **echar una siesta**, **tragar**) para celebrarlo.

4. El incendio fue provocado. ¡Está (**tan blando como el agua**, **tan claro como el agua**, **tan claro como el fuego**)!

5. Comprar una casa es una decisión muy importante; déjame que lo (**consulte con la cama**, **consulte con la almohada**, **oculte la almohada**).

6. Marcos (**sudó la gota delgada**, **sudó la gota gorda**, **escurrió la gota**) en el examen; no tenía ni idea.

7. Lo mejor de todo, es (**cortar todo lo sano**, **extirpar**, **cortar por lo sano**) y acabar de una vez por todas con el problema.

8. (**Por muy buenas y malas**, **Por todo lo malo y lo bueno**, **Por las buenas o por las malas**), hay que convencer a Javier de que siga estudiando.

9. (**Ayer por hoy**, **Hoy por hoy**, **Hay por hay**) sigo pensando en que Luis tuvo la culpa de todo.

10. Manuel es un cabezota, nunca (**tiene un brazo torcido**, **se le tuerce el brazo**, **da su brazo a torcer**).

11. Lo agarraron durmiendo en el trabajo, así que lo (**condecorar**, **van a echar a la calle**, **saldrá a pasear**).

12. El consejo de Ministros se celebró (**con puerta cerrada**, **encerrado**, **a puerta cerrada**).

E. DICTATION
Test Your Aural Comprehension

(This dictation can be found in the Appendix on page 210.)

If you are following along with your cassette, you will now hear a series of sentences from the opening dialogue. These sentences will be read by a native speaker at normal conversational speed (which may seem fast to you at first). In addition, the words will be pronounced as you would actually hear them in a conversation, often including some common reductions.

The first time the sentences are presented, simply listen in order to get accustomed to the speed and heavy use of reductions. The sentences will then be read again with a pause after each to give you time to write down what you heard. The third time the sentences are read, follow along with what you have written.

¡Tengo malas pulgas!

(trans.): **I'm in a lousy mood!**
(lit.): **I have bad fleas!**

¡Tengo malas pulgas!

Isabel: Tengo ganas de comprarme este vestido pero **estoy nadando entre dos aguas**. Además, los precios aquí **están por las nubes** y yo iba a **pagar al contado**. Estoy cansada de tener que **rascarme el bolsillo** cada vez que quiero comprar ropa.

Alma: Estoy de acuerdo contigo. Pero la verdad es que te sienta **como anillo al dedo**. Te lo **digo con el corazón en la mano**, estás guapísima.

Isabel: Si no dejas de **echarme flores**, ¡me voy a **poner colorada**! Bueno. Me has **torcido el brazo**. De hecho, creo que también voy a comprar el bolso, los zapatos, el sombrero y la chaqueta que le hacen juego.

Alma: ¡Tampoco tienes que **echar la casa por la ventana**! ¡Mira! Allí está la vendedora de la que te hablé. La última vez que estuve aquí, me insultó **de buenas a primeras**. ¡Me dijo que yo era gorda! Desde luego **no tiene pelos en la lengua**. Después **nos tiramos de los pelos**. Creo que tengo razón cuando digo que no **tiene don de gentes** y que siempre **tiene malas pulgas**. Yo no sé **qué mosca le ha picado**. Tengo ganas de **cantarle las cuarenta cara a cara**.

Isabel: Ahora le estás **buscando tres pies al gato**. Intenta **morderte la lengua** si viene por aquí. Además, **en el fondo**, a lo mejor es una buena persona con muchos problemas.

Alma: ¡Probablemente **tenga pájaros en la cabeza**! Vamos a **llamar al pan pan y al vino vino**.

Isabel: I feel like buying this dress but I just can't **make up my mind**. Besides, the prices here are **astronomical** and I was going **to pay cash**. I'm so tired of having to **cough up a lot of money** every time I want to buy clothes.

Alma: I know what you mean. But it really **fits you to a T**. **In all honesty**, you look beautiful in it.

Isabel: If you don't stop **flattering me**, you're going to **make me blush**! Okay. You **twisted my arm**. In fact, I think I'll also buy the matching purse, shoes, hat, and jacket.

Alma: You don't have **to go overboard**! Oh, look! There's that saleswoman I was telling you about. The last time I was here, she insulted me **right off the bat**. She told me I was fat! She **doesn't hold any punches**, that's for sure. Then we had a **big fight**. I think it's safe to say that she **doesn't have a way with people** and she's always **irritable**. I don't know **what's bugging her**. I feel like **telling her off right now face to face.**

Isabel: Now you're just **looking for trouble**. Just try and **bite your tongue** if she comes over here. Besides, **deep down** she's probably a good person with a lot of problems.

Alma: She probably has **a screw loose**! Let's **call it like it is**.

I have bad fleas!

Isabel: I feel like buying this dress but I just can't **stop swimming between two waters**. Besides, the prices here are **by the clouds** and I was going **to pay counted**. I'm so tired of having to **scratch my pockets** every time I want to buy clothes.

Alma: I know what you mean. But it really **fits you like a ring to a finger. With the heart in the hand**, you look beautiful in it.

Isabel: If you don't stop **throwing me flowers**, you're going to **put me red**! Okay. You **twisted my arm**. In fact, I think I'll also buy the matching purse, shoes, hat, and jacket.

Alma: You don't have **to throw the house out the window**! Oh, look! There's that saleswoman I was telling you about. The last time I was here, she insulted me **from the good ones to the first ones** by telling me I was fat! She **doesn't have hairs on the tongue**, that's for sure. Then we **pulled from each other's hairs**. I think it's safe to say that she **doesn't have a gift of people** and she always **has bad fleas**. I don't know **what fly bit her**. I feel like **singing the forty truths about her face to face**.

Isabel: Now you're just **looking for three of the cat's feet**. Just try and **bite your tongue** if she comes over here. Besides, **at the bottom** she's probably a good person with a lot of problems.

Alma: She probably has **birds in the head**! Let's **call bread, bread and wine, wine**.

Vocabulary

buscarle tres pies al gato *exp.* to go looking for trouble • (lit.): to look for three of the cat's feet.

> *example:* ¡Relájate! No le **busques tres pies al gato**.
>
> *translation:* Relax! Don't **look for trouble**.
>
> **SYNONYM -1:** **buscarle cinco pies al gato** *exp.* • (lit.): to look for five of the cat's feet.
>
> **SYNONYM -2:** **buscarle mangas al chaleco** *exp.* • (lit.): to look for sleeves in the vest.
>
> **NOTE:** **buscarle los tres pies al gato** *exp. (Cuba)* It's interesting to note that in Cuba, the definite article *los* is used before *tres pies*.

cantarle las cuarenta *exp.* to tell someone off • (lit.): to sing the forty (truths about the person).

> *example:* ¡Estoy harto! ¡Voy a **cantarle las cuarenta**!
>
> *translation:* I'm fed up! I'm going **to tell him off**!
>
> **ALSO -1:** **cantar claro** *exp.* to speak out plainly • (lit.): to sing clearly.
>
> **ALSO -2:** **cantar de plano** *exp.* to make a full confession • (lit.): to sing all of a sudden.
>
> **ALSO -3:** **ser otro cantar** *exp.* to be another story • (lit.): to be another song.

cara a cara *exp.* **1.** right to a person's face • **2.** privately • (lit.): face to face.

> *example:* Me gustaría hablar con Jaime **cara a cara**.
>
> *translation:* I would like to talk to Jaime **privately**.
>
> **SYNONYM:** **frente a frente** *exp.* • (lit.): front to front.
>
> **ALSO -1:** **tener cara dura** *exp.* to have a lot of nerve • (lit.): to have a hard face.

ALSO -2: **dar la cara** *exp.* to face up to things • (lit.): to give face.

ALSO -3: **dar/sacar la cara por uno** *exp.* to stand up for someone, to defend someone • (lit.): to give/stick out the face for someone.

ALSO -4: **poner a mal tiempo buena cara** *exp.* to keep a stiff upper lip • (lit.): to put good face in bad times.

ALSO -5: **poner buena cara a algo** *exp.* to take something well • (lit.): to put good face to something.

ALSO -6: **ser cara dura** *exp.* to be nervy • (lit.): to be a hard face.

ALSO -7: **tener cara de** *exp.* to look • (lit.): to have face of • *tener cara de tristeza;* to look sad.

ALSO -8: **tener cara de pocos amigos** *exp.* to look sad (sour) • (lit.): to have a face of very few friends.

ALSO -9: **tener cara de tonto** *exp.* to look stupid • (lit.): to have a stupid-looking face.

ALSO -10: **tener mucha cara** *exp. (most common in Spain)* to have a lot of nerve • (lit.): to have a lot of face • *Ese tipo tiene mucha cara;* That guy's got a lot of nerve. • *No tengo cara para hacer eso;* I don't have the nerve to do that.

como anillo al dedo (quedar) *exp.* to fit to a T • (lit.): to fit like a ring to a finger.

example: Ese vestido te queda **como anillo al dedo**.

translation: That dress **fits you to a T**.

SYNONYM: **sentar de maravilla** *exp.* • (lit.): to feel wonderful.

con el corazón en la mano *exp.* in all frankness, in all honesty • (lit.): with the heart in the hand.

example: Te lo digo **con el corazón en la mano**. Yo creo que eres muy guapa.

translation: I'm telling you **in all honesty**. I think that you're beautiful.

ALSO -1: **llevar el corazón en la mano** *exp.* to wear one's heart on his sleeve • (lit.): to wear one's heart in one's hand.

ALSO -2: **querer de todo corazón** *exp.* to love with all one's heart • (lit.): [same].

ALSO -3: **ser blado/a [or] duro/a de corazón** *exp.* to be soft [or] hard hearted • (lit.): to be soft [or] hard of heart.

de buenas a primeras *exp.* suddenly (and unexpectedly), right off the bat, from the very start • (lit.): from the good ones to the first ones.

example: Ana me dijo que no quería salir más conmigo **de buenas a primeras**.

translation: Ana told me **right off the bat** she didn't want to go out with me anymore.

SYNONYM -1: **de repente** *exp.* • (lit.): suddenly (of sudden movement).

SYNONYM -2: **luego, luego** *adv. (Mexico)* right away • (lit.): later, later.

NOTE: Although its literal translation is indeed "later, later," when *luego* is repeated twice, it means, oddly enough, "right away, immediately."

ALSO: **bueno/a** *adj.* nasty, bad • (lit.): good • *Tiene una buena gripe;* He/She has a nasty flu.

NOTE: This could be compared to the American expression "to have a real good cold" where "real good" actually refers to something that is negative or unpleasant.

echar flores [a alguien] *exp.* to flatter [someone], to butter [someone] up • (lit.): to throw flowers at someone.

example: No le **eches flores** a Ramón. No va a cambiar de opinión.

translation: Don't **flatter** Ramón. He's not going to change his mind.

SYNONYM -1: **darle la suave a uno** *exp. (Mexico)* • (lit.): to give the soft to someone.

SYNONYM -2: **pasar la mano por el lomo** *exp.* • (lit.): to pass the hand by the back (of an animal).

SYNONYM -3: **pasarle la mano a alguien** *exp.* • (lit.): to pass one's hand to someone.

echar/tirar la casa por la ventana *exp.* to go overboard • (lit.):
to throw the house out the window.

> *example:* ¿Viste cómo Cristina decoró su nueva casa? La verdad
> es que esta vez **echó la casa por la ventana**.

> *translation:* Did you see how Cristina decorated her new house?
> She really **went overboard**.

> **ALSO:** **sentirse como en casa** *exp.* to feel right at home •
> (lit.): to feel like in home.

en el fondo *exp.* deep down, at heart • (lit.): at the bottom.

> *example:* **En el fondo**, Felipe es una buena persona.

> *translation:* **Deep down**, Felipe is a good person.

llamar al pan pan y al vino vino *exp.* to call it like it is • (lit.): to
call bread, bread and wine, wine.

> *example:* Yo siempre **llamo al pan pan y al vino vino**.

> *translation:* I always **call it like it is**.

> **SYNONYM:** **llamar a las cosas por su nombre** *exp.* • (lit.): to
> call things by their name.

morderse la lengua *exp.* to hold or control one's tongue • (lit.): to
bite one's tongue.

> *example:* **¡Muérdete la lengua!**

> *translation:* **Bite your tongue!**

> **ANTONYM -1:** **cantar claro** *exp.* to speak clearly • (lit.): to sing
> clearly.

> **ANTONYM -2:** **no morderse la lengua** *exp.* not to mince words, to
> speak straight from the shoulder • (lit.): not to bite one's
> tongue.

> **ANTONYM -3:** **ser claridoso/a** *exp.* (Venezuela, central America) •
> (lit.): to be very clear.

nadar entre dos aguas *exp.* to be undecided, to be on the fence, not
to be able to make up one's mind • (lit.): to swim between two waters.

> *example:* Roberto no sabe qué coche comprar. Está **nadando
> entre dos aguas**.

translation: Roberto doesn't know what car to buy. He **can't make up his mind**.

SYNONYM -1: **entre azul y buenas noches** *exp.* • (lit.): between blue and a good night.

SYNONYM -2: **ni fu ni fa** *exp. (Spain)* • (lit.): not "fu" nor "fa."

SYNONYM -3: **ni un sí ni un no** *exp.* • (lit.): not a yes nor a no.

no tener pelos en la lengua *exp.* not to mince words, to be outspoken, not to hold back any punches • (lit.): not to have hairs on the tongue.

example: Rafael es una persona muy honesta. **No tiene pelos en la lengua**.

translation: Rafael is a very honest person. **He doesn't hold back any punches**.

ALSO -1: **buscar pelos en la sopa** *exp.* to find fault with everything, to nit-pick • (lit.): to look for hairs in the soup.

ALSO -2: **no tener un pelo de tonto** *exp.* to be nobody's fool • (lit.): not to have a stupid hair.

ALSO -3: **por los pelos** *exp.* by the skin of one's teeth • (lit.): by the hairs.

pagar al contado *exp.* to pay cash • (lit.): to pay counted.

example: Mauricio debe tener mucho dinero porque siempre **paga todo al contado**.

translation: Mauricio must have a lot of money because he always **pays everything in cash**.

SYNONYM -1: **pagar a tocateja** *exp.* • (lit.): to pay tocateja style (no translation for *tocateja*).

SYNONYM -2: **pagar con billete** *exp. (Mexico)* • (lit.): to pay with notes.

SYNONYM -3: **pagar con dinero contante y sonante** *exp.* • (lit.): to pay with money that you can actually count and hear.

poner[se] colorado/a *exp.* to blush, to turn red • (lit.): to put oneself (to become) red.

example: Si sigues hablando así me voy a **poner rojo**.

translation: If you continue to talk like that, I'm going **to turn red**.

VARIATION:	**poner[se] rojo/a** *exp.* • (lit.): to put oneself (to become) red.
SYNONYM:	**acholar[se]** *v. (Ecuador, Peru)* • (lit.): to shame (oneself).
SYNONYM -2:	**ruborizar[se]** *v. (Latin America)* • (lit.): to make oneself blush.

por las nubes (estar) *exp.* astronomical, sky high • (lit.): to be by the clouds.

example: Los precios de esta tienda están **por las nubes**.

translation: Prices at this store are **astronomical**.

ALSO: **en las nubes (estar)** *exp.* to be daydreaming • (lit.): to be in the clouds.

¿Qué mosca te ha picado? *exp.* What's bugging you? • (lit.): What fly has bitten you?

example: No se **qué mosca te ha picado** pero no me gusta cuando estás de mal humor.

translation: I don't know **what's eating you**, but I don't like it when you are in such a bad mood.

SYNONYM: ¿Qué bicho te ha picado? *exp.* • (lit.): What bug has bitten you?

rascarse el bolsillo *exp.* to cough up money • (lit.): to scratch one's pocket.

example: Estoy cansado de **rascarme el bolsillo** para pagar la renta cada mes. A lo mejor es hora de que compre una casa.

translation: I'm tired of **coughing up money** every month on rent. Maybe it's time for me to buy a house.

tener don de gentes *exp.* to have a way with people • (lit.): to have a gift of people.

example: Estefanía **tiene don de gentes**.

translation: Estefania **has a way with people**.

tener malas pulgas *exp.* to be irritable, ill-tempered • (lit.): to have bad fleas.

> *example:* José siempre **tiene malas pulgas**.
>
> *translation:* Jose is always so **irritable**.
>
> **SYNONYM -1:** **tener mal humor** *exp.* • (lit.): to have bad humor or mood.
>
> **SYNONYM -2:** **tener un humor de perros** *exp.* • (lit.): to have a mood of dogs.
>
> **SEE:** **de un humor de perros (estar)**, *p. 140.*

tener pájaros en la cabeza *exp.* to be crazy, to have a screw lose • (lit.): to have birds in the head.

> *example:* Daniel **tiene pájaros en la cabeza**.
>
> *translation:* Daniel **has a screw lose**.
>
> **SYNONYM -1:** **estar como una cabra** *exp.* • (lit.): to be like a goat.
>
> **SYNONYM -2:** **estar loco/a de remate** *exp.* • (lit.): to be crazy in the end.
>
> **SYNONYM -3:** **estar tocado/a** *exp. (Spain)* • (lit.): to be touched.
>
> **SYNONYM -4:** **faltar un tornillo** *exp.* (lit.): to have a screw missing.

tirarse/jalarse de los pelos *exp.* to squabble, to have a fight (either verbally or physically) • (lit.): to pull from one's hairs.

> *example:* Verónica y Luis se estaban **tirando de los pelos**.
>
> *translation:* Veronica and Luis were **having a big fight**.
>
> **NOTE:** The verb *jalarse* is used primarily in Mexico.

torcer el brazo de alguien *exp.* to convince someone to do something, to twist someone's arm • (lit.): to twist one's arm.

> *example:* Bueno, **me has torcido el brazo**. Mañana te ayudo a limpiar la casa.
>
> *translation:* Well, **you twisted my arm**. Tomorrow I'll help you do some house cleaning.
>
> **SEE:** **dar el brazo a torcer**, *p. 45.*

Practice the Vocabulary

(Answers to Lesson Four, p. 196)

A. Choose the letter which corresponds to the correct definition of the words in boldface.

1. **cantarle las cuarenta**:
   a. to sing in the style of the 1940's
   b. to tell him/her off

2. **poner colorado/a**:
   a. to make someone blush
   b. to get a suntan

3. **tener pájaros en la cabeza**:
   a. to be intelligent
   b. to have a screw loose

4. **estar por las nubes**:
   a. astronomical prices
   b. cheap

5. **pagar al contado**:
   a. to count money
   b. to pay cash

6. **decir algo con el corazón en la mano**:
   a. to say something in all honesty
   b. to lie

7. **echarse flores**:
   a. to feel inferior
   b. to flatter oneself

8. **de buenas a primeras**:
    a. right at the end
    b. right off the bat

9. **no tener pelos en la lengua**:
    a. to be very hairy
    b. to tell the truth without hesitation

10. **tener don de gentes**:
    a. to have a way with people
    b. not to get along with people

11. **llamar al pan pan y al vino vino**:
    a. to be hungry and thirsty
    b. to call it like it is

12. **en el fondo**:
    a. deep down
    b. superficially

B. Fill in the following blanks with the letter that corresponds to the best answer.

1. ¡Qué barbaridad! Los precios de esta tienda están _____.
    a. **por el sol**
    b. **grandes**
    c. **por las nubes**

2. Cada vez que vamos a algún sitio, soy yo el que tiene que
    _____.
    a. **abrillantar el bolso**
    b. **limpiar el bolsillo**
    c. **rascarse el bolsillo**

3. Eva le viene _____ a Alfredo
    a. **como anillo al dedo**
    b. **muy grande la falda**
    c. **todos los días con**

4. Olga sólo decidió _____ cuando le tocó la lotería.
   a. **abren las ventanas de la casa**
   b. **echar la ventana por la casa**
   c. **echar la casa por la ventana**

5. Juan no para de _____, es un creído.
   a. **comprar flores**
   b. **echarse flores**
   c. **florecer**

6. Mónica tiene _____, siempre está de mal humor.
   a. **muy malas pulgas**
   b. **muchas pulgas**
   c. **un saco de pulgas**

7. No sé _____, pero últimamente estás insoportable.
   a. **cuántas moscas hay**
   b. **qué mosca te ha picado**
   c. **nada de él**

8. Me gustaría decirle _____ lo mucho que le quiero.
   a. **que es muy caro**
   b. **cara dura**
   c. **cara a cara**

9. Estuve a punto de contarle todo, pero al final logré _____.
   a. **morderme la lengua**
   b. **masticarme la lengua**
   c. **aprender una lengua**

10. Andrés siempre le _____, es incorregible.
    a. **gustan los pies del gato**
    b. **busca siete vidas al gato**
    c. **busca tres pies al gato**

11. Ana siempre _____, es una sentimental
    a. **tiene corazones en las manos**
    b. **dice las cosas con el corazón en la mano**
    c. **come con las manos**

12. _____ es muy buena persona, pero le cuesta demostrarlo.
    a. **Por arriba**
    b. **En el fondo**
    c. **Al fondo**

C. Match the English phrase in the left column with the Spanish translation from the right. Mark the appropriate letter in the box.

☐ 1. I can't make up my mind.

☐ 2. Prices of real estate in Madrid are astronomical.

☐ 3. Their children are always fighting.

☐ 4. She told him the truth face to face.

☐ 5. That coat really fits him well.

☐ 6. He got angry right off the bat.

☐ 7. I don't want to go. Please stop twisting my arm.

☐ 8. Jaime is such a big spender. He always goes overboard.

☐ 9. Marta always speaks in all honesty.

☐ 10. Carlos has a screw loose.

☐ 11. Ana is very shy. She blushes easily.

☐ 12. Having a way with people is an excellent human quality.

A. Sus niños están siempre **tirándose de los pelos**.

B. Ese abrigo le viene **como anillo al dedo**.

C. No quiero ir; **no me tuerzas el brazo**.

D. Los precios de la vivienda en Madrid **están por las nubes**.

E. Jaime es un derrochador. Siempre está **echando la casa por la ventana**.

F. Ana es muy tímida. **Se pone colorada** enseguida.

G. Carlos **tiene pájaros en la cabeza**.

H. **Tener don de gentes** es una cualidad excelente.

I. Estoy **nadando entre dos aguas**.

J. Se enfadó **de buenas a primeras**.

K. Ella le dijo la verdad **cara a cara**.

L. Marta siempre dice las cosas **con el corazón en la mano**.

D. FIND-A-WORD PUZZLE
Using the list below, circle the words in the grid on page 73 that are missing from the Spanish idiom. Words may be spelled up, down, or across.

aguas	don	nubes
anillo	flores	pájaros
bolsillo	fondo	pelos
brazo	gato	primeras
cara	lengua	pulgas
contado	mano	rojo
cuarenta	mosca	ventana

1. *example:* No sabe qué coche comprar. Está **nadando entre dos _____**.

    translation: He doesn't know what car to buy. He **can't make up his mind**.

2. *example:* Los precios de esta tienda están **por las _____**.

    translation: Prices at this store are **astronomical**.

3. *example:* Mauricio debe tener mucho dinero porque siempre **paga todo al _____**.

    translation: Mauricio must have a lot of money because he always **pays everything in cash**.

4. *example:* A Manuel no le gusta **rascarse el _____**.

    translation: Manuel doesn't like **to cough up money**.

5. *example:* Ese vestido te queda **como _____ al dedo**.

    translation: That dress **fits you to a T**.

6.   *example:*   Te lo digo **con el corazón en la** _____. Yo creo que eres muy guapa.

     translation: I'm telling you **in all honesty**. I think you are beautiful.

7.   *example:*   No le **eches** _____ a Ramón. No va a cambiar de opinión.

     translation: Don't **flatter** Ramón. He's not going to change his mind.

8.   *example:*   Si sigues hablando así me voy a **poner** _____.

     translation: If you continue to talk like that, I'm going **to turn red**.

9.   *example:*   Bueno, **me has torcido el** _____. Mañana te ayudo a limpiar la casa.

     translation: Well, **you twisted my arm**. Tomorrow I'll help you do some house cleaning.

10.   *example:*   Parece que Cristina **tiró la casa por la** _____.

     translation: It looks like Cristina **went overboard**.

11.   *example:*   Ana me dijo que no quería salir más conmigo **de buenas a** _____.

     translation: Ana told me **right off the bat** she didn't want to go out with me anymore.

12.   *example:*   Rafael es una persona muy honesta. **No tiene pelos en la** _____.

     translation: Rafael is a very honest person. **He doesn't hold back any punches**.

13. *example:* Verónica y Luis se estaban **tirando de los** _____.

    translation: Veronica and Luis were **having a big fight**.

14. *example:* Estefanía **tiene** _____ **de gentes**.

    translation: Estefania **has a way with people**.

15. *example:* José siempre **tiene malas** _____.

    translation: Jose is always so **irritable**.

16. *example:* No se **qué** _____ **te ha picado** pero no me gusta cuando estás de mal humor.

    translation: I don't know **what's eating you**, but I don't like it when you are in such a bad mood.

17. *example:* ¡Estoy harto! ¡Voy a **cantarle las** _____!

    translation: I'm fed up! I'm going **to tell him off**!

18. *example:* Me gustaría hablar con Jaime **cara a** _____.

    translation: I would like to talk to Jaime **privately**.

19. *example:* ¡Relájate! No le **busques tres pies al** _____.

    translation: Relax! Don't **look for trouble**.

20. *example:* **En el** _____ Felipe es una buena persona.

    translation: **Deep down**, Felipe is a good person.

21. *example:* Daniel **tiene** _____ **en la cabeza**.

    translation: Daniel **has a screw lose**.

FIND-A-WORD PUZZLE

```
L E N G U A E L M P G W
T A L O G O N E B R A T
M M N O W I C D O I Z R
A A U M A G P M L M P A
M V B A N W E U S E A S
A E E N A A L R I R C T
G N S G T F O P L A H O
U T L A S L S O L S O A
A A S N O O M L O M T N
S N C I M R S I L N G A
C A U L E E E S E G F D
H H E L D S M R O D O O
I P C O N T A D O O N H
C Á T A L U I I S W D O
O J I U C U C S E N O W
C A R A N P U L G A S R
B R A Z O M A D G A R O
Z O A I G A T O M M M J
P S M O S C A N R A D O
```

E. DICTATION
Test Your Aural Comprehension

(This dictation can be found in the Appendix on page 210.)

If you are following along with your cassette, you will now hear a series of sentences from the opening dialogue. These sentences will be read by a native speaker at normal conversational speed (which may seem fast to you at first). In addition, the words will be pronounced as you would actually hear them in a conversation, often including some common reductions.

The first time the sentences are presented, simply listen in order to get accustomed to the speed and heavy use of reductions. The sentences will then be read again with a pause after each to give you time to write down what you heard. The third time the sentences are read, follow along with what you have written.

Es un *hueso duro de roer.*

(trans.): She's a **tough nut to crack**.
(lit.): She's a **hard bone to chew**.

Es un hueso duro de roer

Carlos: ¿Ya conociste a tus nuevos vecinos?

Mario: Sí. Se llaman Inés y Antonio. **De una vez por todas**, decidí ir allí y **romper el hielo**. La verdad es que **empezamos con buen pie**. Me **hice amigo de** ellos en seguida. Me dieron la bienvenida **con los brazos abiertos**, no como la última señora que vivió allí. ¿Recuerdas cómo **me dio un portazo en las narices** cuando fui allí a presentarme? Verdaderamente era **un hueso duro de roer**.

Carlos: Bueno, **vayamos al asunto**. Cuéntamelo todo **sin faltar una coma**.

Mario: Bueno, al principio **me sentí como pez en el agua**. Pero entonces Inés empezó a **echar espumarajos** porque Antonio no estaba **moviendo un dedo** y ella estaba haciendo todo el trabajo de desempacar. Entonces, empezaron a **gritar como unos descosidos**. La verdad es que **perdieron los estribos**. Así que les dije que si querían que les **echara una mano**. Debo admitir que al principio **hicieron mal papel**. Pero después de unos momentos, **saltaba a la vista** que todo esto lo provocó el stress* de estar en una casa nueva. No creo que la mudanza salió **a pedir de boca**. Pero **al fin y al cabo** todo saldrá bien.

Carlos: Así que, ¿cómo son?

Mario: Inés dice que tiene treinta años pero me **cuesta trabajo** creérlo. Yo creo que **se quita unos años**. Yo también pienso que ella **lleva los pantalones**. Antonio **no inventó la pólvora**, pero parece ser buena persona. Ella acaba de **dar a luz a** una bebé que es la **misma imagen** que Inés.

Indeed, the English word "stress" is used in many Spanish-speaking countries.

Lesson Five

Carlos: Did you meet your new neighbors yet?

Mario: Yes. Their names are Inez and Antonio. **Once and for all**, I decided to go over and **break the ice**. We really **got off to a good start**. I **made friends with them** right away. They welcomed me **with open arms**, not like the last woman who lived there. Remember how she **slammed the door in my face** when I went over to introduce myself? She was really a **tough nut to crack**.

Carlos: Okay. Let's **get down to facts**. Tell me everything **down to the last detail**.

Mario: Well, at first I **felt right at home**. But then Inez got **ticked off** because Antonio wasn't **lifting a finger** and she was stuck doing all the unpacking herself. Then they started **shouting at the top of their lungs**. They really **lost it**. So, I offered to **give them a hand**. I have to admit that at first, they made a **bad impression** on me. But after a few moments it was **obvious** that it was just the stress of being in a new home. I don't think the move **went smoothly**. But I'm sure **when the dust clears**, everything will be fine.

Carlos: So, what are they like?

Mario: Ines says she's thirty years old but I **had trouble** swallowing that. I think she **lies about her age**. I also think she **wears the pants in the family**. Antonio **isn't very bright** but he seems like a nice guy. And they just **gave birth to** a baby girl who is the **spitting image** of Ines.

She's a hard bone to chew

Carlos: Did you meet your new neighbors yet?

Mario: Yes. Their names are Inez and Antonio. **For one time and for all**, I decided to go over and **break the ice**. We really **began with a good foot**. I **made friends of them** right away. They welcomed me **with open arms**, not like the last woman who lived there. Remember how she **gave a slam in my nose** when I went over to introduce myself? She was really a **hard bone to chew**.

Carlos: Okay. Let's **go to the subject**. Tell me everything **without missing a comma**.

Mario: Well, at first I **felt like a fish in water**. But then Inez started **throwing foam from the mouth** because Antonio wasn't **moving a finger** and she was stuck doing all the unpacking herself. Then they started **screaming like something unstiched**. They really **lost the stirrups**. So, I offered to **throw them a hand**. I have to admit that at first, they did a **bad theatrical role** on me. But after a few moments it **jumped to the sight** that it was just the stress of being in a new home. I don't think the move **tasted from the mouth**. But I'm sure **to the end and to the end**, everything will be fine.

Carlos: So, what are they like?

Mario: Ines says she's thirty years old but it **costs work** to believe it. I think she **takes off years**. I also think she **wears the pants**. Antonio **didn't invent gunpowder** but he seems like a nice guy. And they just **gave light to** a baby girl who is the **same image** of Ines.

Vocabulary

a pedir de boca *exp.* smoothly • (lit.): to taste from the mouth.

> *example:* Esta presentación me ha salido **a pedir de boca**.

> *translation:* This presentation **went smoothly**.

> **NOTE:** This popular expression can also be used in the culinary world when a dish has been prepared to perfection meaning "delicious" or "perfect" • *Esta langosta está a pedir de boca;* This lobster is delicious.

al fin y al cabo *exp.* after all, when the dust clears • (lit.): to the end and to the end.

> *example:* **Al fin y al cabo** todo salió bien.

> *translation:* **When all was said and done**, everything turned out okay.

como pez en el agua (sentirse) *exp.* to feel right at home • (lit.): to feel like a fish in water.

> *example:* Estoy muy contento. **Me siento como pez en el agua**.

> *translation:* I'm so happy. **I feel right at home**.

> **SYNONYM:** **como Pedro por su casa (andar)** *exp.* • (lit.): like Pedro in his house.

> **ANTONYM -1:** **como [un] pez fuera del agua (estar)** *exp.* to feel out of place, to feel like a fish out of water • (lit.): to be like a fish out of water.

> **ANTONYM -2:** **como gallina en corral ajeno (estar)** *exp.* • (lit.): to be like a chicken in a strange pen.

> **ANTONYM -3:**   **como perro en barrio ajeno (estar)** *exp.* • (lit.): to be like a dog in a strange neighborhood.

con los brazos abiertos *exp.* with open arms.

> *example:*   Cuando Juan volvió de la guerra, le recibimos **con los brazos abiertos**.
>
> *translation:*   When Juan came back from the war, we welcomed him **with open arms**.
>
> **ALSO:**   **estar hecho un brazo de mar** *exp.* to be dressed to kill • (lit.): to be made an arm to the sea.

costar trabajo hacer algo *exp.* to have trouble believing/ swallowing something • (lit.): to cost work.

> *example:*   **Me cuesta trabajo** creer que Pedro ganó la apuesta.
>
> *translation:*   **I have trouble** believing that Pedro won the bet.

dar a luz a *exp.* to give birth to • (lit.): to give light to.

> *example:*   Marta **dio a luz a** una preciosa niña.
>
> *translation:*   Marta **gave birth to a** beautiful girl.

dar un portazo *exp.* to slam the door • (lit.): to give a slam (of a door).

> *example:*   ¡No **des portazos** por favor!
>
> *translation:*   Please don't **slam the door**!
>
> **SYNONYM:**   **tirar la puerta** *exp.* • (lit.): to throw the door.

de una vez por todas *exp.* once and for all • (lit.): for one time and for all.

> *example:*   Voy a terminar este proyecto **de una vez por todas**.
>
> *translation:*   I'm going to finish this project **once and for all**.
>
> **SYNONYM -1:**   **de una vez** *exp.* • (lit.): for one time.

SYNONYM -2:   **de una vez y para siempre** *exp.* • (lit.): for one time and for always.

echar espumarajos [por la boca] *exp.* to be furious, to foam at the mouth with rage • (lit.): to throw foam [from the mouth].

> *example:*   Rafael está **echando espumarajos [por la boca]** porque le robaron su coche.
>
> *translation:*   Rafael is furious **because somebody stole his car.**

SYNONYM -1:   **echar humo** *exp.* • (lit.): to throw smoke (in the air).

SYNONYM -2:   **enchilarse** *v. (Mexico)* • (lit.): to get red in the face from eating chilies.

echar una mano a alguien *exp.* to lend someone a hand • (lit.): to throw someone a hand.

> *example:*   Voy a **echarle una mano** a Juan con esas cajas.
>
> *translation:*   I'm going **to lend** Juan **a hand** Juan with those boxes.

SYNONYM -1:   **dar una mano a alguien** *exp.* • (lit.): to give someone a hand.

SYNONYM -2:   **echar la mano a alguien** *exp.* • (lit.): to throw the hand to someone.

empezar con buen pie *exp.* to get off to a good start • (lit.): to begin with a good foot.

> *example:*   Esta mañana gané la lotería. **Empecé con buen pie**.
>
> *translation:*   I won the lottery this morning. **I got off to a good start**.

gritar como unos descosidos *exp.* to scream one's lungs out, to scream out of control • (lit.): to scream like something unstiched.

> *example:*   Cuando fuimos al restaurante, mis niños estaban **gritando como unos descosidos**.

translation: When we went to the restaurant, my kids were **screaming out of control**.

NOTE: This expression comes from the verb *descoser* meaning "to unstitch." Therefore, this expression could be loosely translated as "to come apart at the seams."

ALSO: **beber/comer/correr como un descosido** *exp.* to drink/eat/run like crazy • (lit.): to drink/eat/run like something unstitched.

hacer mal/buen papel *exp.* to make a bad/good impression • (lit.): to do a bad/good (theatrical) role.

example: **Hiciste un buen papel** anoche.

translation: **You made a good impression** last night.

SYNONYM: **caer mal/bien** *exp.* • (lit.): to fall badly/well.

hacer[se] amigo de *exp.* to make friends with • (lit.): to make friends of.

example: **Me hice amigo de** Pedro porque es muy simpático.

translation: **I made friends with** Pedro because he's very nice.

SYNONYM: **hacer buenas migas con** *exp.* • (lit.): to make good bread crumbs with.

ir al asunto *exp.* to get down to the facts • (lit.): to go to the subject.

example: ¡**Vamos al asunto**!

translation: **Let's get down to the facts**!

llevar los pantalones *exp.* to wear the pants, to be in command • (lit.): to wear the pants.

example: En mi casa yo **llevo los pantalones**.

translation: In my house, **I wear the pants in the family**.

SYNONYM -1: **llevar los calzones** *exp.* • (lit.): to wear underwear.

SYNONYM -2: **llevar la batuta** *exp.* • (lit.): to carry the baton.

misma imagen (ser la) *exp.* to be the spitting image of • (lit.): to be the same image.

> *example:* David es **la misma imagen** que su padre.

> *translation:* David is the **spitting image** of his father.

> **SYNONYM -1:** **ser escupido/a de** *exp.* • (lit.): to be the spit of.

> **SYNONYM -2:** **ser viva imagen de** *exp.* • (lit.): to be the live image of.

no inventar la pólvora *exp.* not to be very bright • (lit.): not to invent gunpowder.

> *example:* Mauricio **no ha inventado la pólvora**.

> *translation:* Mauricio **is not very bright**.

> **SYNONYM -1:** **no estar muy despierto/a** *exp.* • (lit.): not to be very awake.

> **SYNONYM -2:** **no ser muy vivo/a** *exp.* *(Mexico)* • (lit.): not to be very alive.

no mover un dedo *exp.* not to lift a finger • (lit.): not to move a finger.

> *example:* Andrés **nunca mueve un dedo**.

> *translation:* Andrés **never lifts a finger**.

> **SYNONYM:** **no levantar un dedo** *exp.* • (lit.): not to lift a finger.

perder los estribos *exp.* to lose control, to lose one's head, to lose one's temper • (lit.): to lose the stirrups.

> *example:* Como sigas portándote así, voy a **perder los estribos**.

> *translation:* If you continue to behave this way, I'm going to **lose my temper**.

> **SYNONYM -1:** **perder la calma** *exp.* • (lit.): to lose one's calm.

> **SYNONYM -2:** **perder la paciencia** *exp.* • to lose one's patience.

quitarse años *exp.* to lie about one's age • (lit.): to take off years.

> *example:* Teresa siempre **se quita años**.
>
> *translation:* Teresa always **lies about her age**.

romper el hielo *exp.* to break the ice • (lit.): to break the ice.

> *example:* Hice una broma para **romper el hielo**.
>
> *translation:* I told a joke **to break the ice**.
>
> **ALSO:** **estar hecho/a un hielo** *exp.* to be frozen, to be freezing cold • (lit.): to be made an ice.

saltar a la vista *exp.* to be obvious • (lit.): to jump to the sight.

> *example:* **Salta a la vista** que Pepe hace ejercicio diariamente.
>
> *translation:* **It's obvious** that Pepe exercises daily.
>
> **SYNONYM:** **saltar a los ojos** *exp.* • (lit.): to jump to the eyes.

sin faltar una coma *exp.* down to the last detail • (lit.): without missing a comma.

> *example:* Te voy a contar lo que pasó **sin faltar una coma**.
>
> *translation:* I'm going to tell you what happened **down to the last detail**.
>
> **SYNONYM:** **con puntos y comas** *exp.* • (lit.): with periods and commas.

un hueso duro de roer (ser) *exp.* to be a tough nut to crack • (lit.): to be a hard bone to chew.

> *example:* No pude convencer al jefe para que me diera un aumento. Es **un hueso duro de roer**.
>
> *translation:* I couldn't convince the boss to give me a raise. He's **a tough nut to crack**.

Practice the Vocabulary

(Answers to Lesson Five, p. 197)

A. Fill in the blank with the correct word(s) using the list below.

a pedir de boca	**misma imagen**
con los brazos abiertos	**mover un dedo**
cuesta mucho trabajo	**pierde los estribos**
dar a luz	**quita años**
echaras una mano	**salta a la vista**
hice amigo de	**vayamos al asunto**

1. Nos recibió _____.

2. Felipe es la _____ de su padre.

3. Me _____ Jorge enseguida.

4. Cuando llegué al hospital, Beatriz acababa de _____ a un niño precioso.

5. Estoy ocupadísimo; me vendría muy bien que me _____ en el trabajo.

6. No estoy dispuesto a _____ por él porque se portó muy mal conmigo.

7. Mi jefe _____ muy fácilmente. Tiene un carácter fuerte.

8. A pesar de conservarse muy bien, Ana siempre se _____.

9. El último examen que hice me salió _____.

10. Ya estoy cansada de darle vueltas, _____.

11. Lisa y Mark siempre van agarrados de la mano, _____ que están enamorados.

12. Los lunes por la mañana me _____ madrugar.

B. Underline the appropriate word(s) that best complete(s) the phrase.

1. No lo dudes más; cásate (**de una vez por todas**, **por todas las veces**, **de todas**).

2. ¡Cuéntame todos los detalles de tu viaje, (**sin que te coma**, **sobre una coma**, **sin faltar una coma**)!

3. Deberíamos cenar todos juntos esta noche, (**al fin y al cabo**, **al final**, **por fin acabo**) es Nochebuena.

4. En casa, la que realmente (**usa pantalones**, **lleva la falda**, **lleva los pantalones**), es mi madre.

5. Me gustaría no (**papel malo**, **hacer un mal papel**, **tener mal papel**) el día de mi graduación.

6. Me siento (**como pez de agua dulce**, **en una pecera**, **como pez en el agua**) en mi oficina.

7. Pedro es un (**hueso duro de roer**, **roedor de huesos**, **hueso muy roído**), nunca se deja convencer.

8. Cuando me negaron el préstamo, sentí como si me (**dieran una puerta**, **dieran un portazo**, **se cerrara una ventana**).

9. Este año (**tuvimos buenos pies**, **decidimos empezar los pies**, **empezamos con buen pie**); el uno de enero nos tocó la lotería.

10. María es un poco histérica, cada vez que ve una película de miedo, grita (**como una descosida**, **desfondadamente**, **como un pantalón desfondado).**

11. Los Rolling Stones (**helaron los rotos**, **se rompen los hielos**, **rompieron el hielo**) en los primeros compases del concierto.

12. Cuando Manuel se enfada, (**echa espumarajos**, **echa aguas**, **echa esponjas**) de todo el mundo.

C. Match the English phrase in the left column with the Spanish translation from the right. Mark the appropriate letter in the box.

1. John wasn't too bright when he said that winters aren't very cold in Alaska.

2. If you gave me a hand, I'd finish my homework right away.

3. Antonio is the laziest person I've ever known. He never lifts a finger to do housework.

4. The Johnsons are very nice. They welcomed me with open arms.

5. Maria gave birth to a beautiful baby girl last week.

6. Every time I go to the mountains, I feel right at home.

7. Jorge is the spitting image of his father.

8. It is obvious that Monica is a lot smarter than Marta.

9. Tell me once and for all what you feel like doing today.

10. Maria is the one that wears the pants in the family; she has a strong personality.

11. Stop beating around the bush and get straight to the point.

12. Jorge and Maria became friends right after they met.

A. María **dio a luz a** una niña preciosa la semana pasada.

B. Cada vez que voy a las montañas, **me siento como pez en el agua**.

C. Deja ya de **dar rodeos** y ve directo al asunto.

D. John **no inventó la pólvora** cuando dijo que los inviernos no son fríos en Alaska.

E. Jorge y María **se hicieron amigos** nada más conocerse.

F. Si me **echaras una mano**, terminaría mi tarea enseguida.

G. Los Johnsons son muy simpáticos, me recibieron **con los brazos abiertos**.

H. María es la que **lleva los pantalones** en casa, tiene mucho carácter.

I. Antonio es la persona más vaga que he conocido. Nunca **mueve un dedo** en el trabajo de la casa.

J. Dime de **una vez por todas** qué te apetece hacer hoy.

K. Jorge es **la misma imagen de** su padre.

L. **Salta a la vista** que Mónica es mucho más inteligente que Marta.

D. Complete the dialogue using the list below.

a pedir de boca
al fin y al cabo
con los brazos abiertos
cuesta trabajo
dar a luz
de una vez por todas
descosidos
echar espumarajos
echara una mano
empezamos con buen pie
gritar como unos *descosidos*
hice amigo de
hicieron mal papel
lleva los pantalones

me sentí como pez en
   el agua
me dio un portazo en
   las narices
misma imagen
moviendo un dedo
no inventó la pólvora
perdieron los estribos
romper el hielo
saltaba a la vista
se quita unos años
sin faltar una coma
un hueso duro de roer
vayamos al asunto

Carlos: ¿Ya conociste a tus nuevos vecinos?

Mario: Sí. Se llaman Inés y Antonio. _____,

decidí ir allí y _____. La verdad es que

_____. Me _____ ellos en

seguida. Me dieron la bienvenida _____,

no como la última señora que vivió allí. ¿Recuerdas cómo

_____ cuando fui allí a presentarme?

Verdaderamente era _____.

Carlos: Bueno, _____. Cuéntamelo todo

_____.

Mario: Bueno, al principio _____. Pero

entonces Inés empezó a _____ porque

Antonio no estaba _____ y ella estaba

haciendo todo el trabajo de desempacar. Entonces, empezaron a

_____. La verdad es que

_____. Así que les dije que si

querían que les _____. Debo admitir que

al principio _____. Pero después de

unos momentos, _____ que todo

esto lo provocó el "stress" de estar en una casa nueva. No creo

que la mudanza salió _____. Pero

_____ todo saldrá bien.

Carlos: Así que, ¿cómo son?

Mario: Inés dice que tiene treinta años pero me _____

tragármelo. Yo creo que _____. Yo también

pienso que ella _____. Antonio

_____, pero parece ser buena

persona. Ella acaba de _____ una bebé que

es la _____ que Inés.

E. DICTATION
Test Your Aural Comprehension

(This dictation can be found in the Appendix on page 211.)

If you are following along with your cassette, you will now hear a series of sentences from the opening dialogue. These sentences will be read by a native speaker at normal conversational speed (which may seem fast to you at first). In addition, the words will be pronounced as you would actually hear them in a conversation, often including some common reductions.

The first time the sentences are presented, simply listen in order to get accustomed to the speed and heavy use of reductions. The sentences will then be read again with a pause after each to give you time to write down what you heard. The third time the sentences are read, follow along with what you have written.

REVIEW EXAM FOR LESSONS 1-5

(Answers to Review, p. 199)

A. Underline the correct definition of the slang word(s) in boldface.

1. **poner colorado/a**:
   a. to make someone blush
   b. to get a suntan

2. **ser todo oídos**:
   a. to be all ears
   b. to have big ears

3. **para chuparse los dedos**:
   a. delicious
   b. terrible

4. **hablar por los codos**:
   a. to talk slowly
   b. to talk someone's ear off

5. **quedarse mudo**:
   a. to close one's eyes
   b. to be speechless

6. **llamar al pan pan y al vino vino**:
   a. to be hungry and thirsty
   b. to call it like it is

7. **ahogarse en un vaso de agua**:
   a. to enjoy swimming
   b. to make a mountain out of a mole hill

8. **de tal palo, tal astilla**:
   a. to hurt someone with a stick
   b. like father like son

9. **sobre gustos no hay nada escrito**:
   a. everyone has his/her own taste
   b. to enjoy writing

10. **tomar el pelo a alguien**:
    a. to pull someone's leg
    b. to cut someone's hair

11. **mucho ruido y pocas nueces**:
    b. to be very loud
    a. a big deal about nothing

12. **tener pájaros en la cabeza**:
    a. to be very smart.
    b. to have a screw loose

13. **consultarlo con la almohada**:
    a. to talk to a doctor
    b. to sleep on it

14. **estar hasta la coronilla**:
    a. to be fed up
    b. to wear a crown

15. **estar por las nubes**:
    a. astronomical prices
    b. inexpensive

16. **dar a luz a**:

    a. to give birth to

    b. to turn the light on

17. **tan claro como el agua**:

    a. clear water

    b. to be plain as day

18. **romper el hielo**:

    a. to break the ice

    b. to be cold as ice

19. **echarse flores**:

    a. to buy oneself gifts

    b. to flatter yourself

20. **estar como pez en el agua**:

    a. to go sailing

    b. to feel right at home

21. **ser uña y carne**:

    a. to be inseparable

    b. to be intelligent

22. **ser la misma imagen**:

    a. to be the spitting image of

    b. to take a picture

23. **no tener pelos en la lengua**:

    a. to be very hairy

    b. to tell the truth without hesitation

B. Complete the following phrases by choosing the appropriate word(s) from the list below.

anda de boca en boca mala espina ✻₁
da su brazo a torcer por las nubes
estaba de moda   puso al corriente
hacer un mal papel tan claro como el agua
hasta la coronilla tengo en la punta de la lengua
hoy por hoy   tiene madera de

1. El detective _____ de todo a la policía.

2. La noticia ya _____; lo sabe todo el mundo.

3. Pedro es un cabezota, nunca _____.

4. En fin de año el precio de las uvas estaba _____.

5. No quisiera _____ el día de tu boda.

6. _____ sigo pensando que Jaime tuvo la culpa de todo.

7. Este niño _____ futbolista.

8. Lo _____, pero no puedo acordarme.

9. Estoy _____ de Paco, siempre está haciendo gamberradas.

10. Está _____; el incendio fue provocado.

11. Le dio _____ que negara todo.

12. En los años 60 _____ el pelo largo.

C. Match the English phrase in the left column with the Spanish translation from the right. Mark the appropriate letter in the box.

1. My wife is the one who really wears the pants at home.

2. Stop beating around the bush and get straight to the point.

3. Maria gave birth to a beautiful baby girl last week.

4. Teresa has a reputation of being a cheapskate.

5. Olga is crazy.

6. Marcos is wild about his son.

7. Ana is very shy. She blushes easily.

8. Having a way with people is an excellent human quality.

9. When he realized how much it was going to cost, he hit the ceiling.

10. It's easier said than done.

11. The meeting was held behind closed doors.

12. That dress really fits her to a "T".

A. La reunión se celebró **a puerta cerrada**.

B. A Marcos **se le cae la baba** por su hijo.

C. **Del dicho al hecho hay mucho trecho**.

D. Deja ya de **dar rodeos** y ve directo al asunto.

E. Cuando se dio cuenta de lo que le iba a costar **puso el grito en el cielo**.

F. Ese vestido **le sienta como anillo al dedo**.

G. María **dio a luz a** una niña preciosa la semana pasada.

H. A Olga **le falta un tornillo**.

I. **Tener don de gentes** es una cualidad excelente.

J. Teresa **tiene fama de** tacaña.

K. Mi esposa es la que realmente **lleva los pantalones** en casa.

L. Ana es muy tímida, **se pone colorada** enseguida.

D. Underline the appropriate word(s) that best complete(s) the phrase.

1. ¡Venga, cuéntame! (**tengo un oído**, **soy todo oídos**, **oigo bien**).

2. En cuanto se enteró de la noticia, Manuel llegó al hospital (**muy tarde**, **en menos que canta un gallo**, **me encantan los gallos**).

3. Me enfadé con Salvador porque me (**dobló la esquina**, **se dio contra la esquína**, **me dio esquinazo**).

4. Cristina dice todo lo que piensa, es (**muy rápida**, **muy ligera de palabras**, **las palabras**).

5. Cuando Alejandro se enfada, pierde el control y (**lava los trapos siempre**, **pone los trapos a remojar**, **pone a todo el mundo como un trapo**).

6. Manuel es un cabezota, nunca (**tiene un brazo torcido**, **se le tuerce el brazo**, **da su brazo a torcer**).

7. Los profesores tuvieron una reunión (**a puerta caída**, **encerrada**, **a puerta cerrada**).

8. (**Por muy buenas y malas**, **Por todo lo malo y lo bueno**, **Por las buenas o por las malas**), hay que convencer a Javier de que siga estudiando.

9. ¡Incluya en el informe todos los detalles de su reunión, (**sin que le coma**, **sobre una coma**, **sin faltar una coma**)!

10. Este año (**tuvimos buenos pies**, **decidimos empezar los pies**, **empezamos con buen pie**); el uno de enero nos tocó la lotería.

11. Alfonso (**tiene fama de**, **es famoso**, **tiene hambre**) de guapo.

12. ¡(**Hoy por hoy**, **Mañana por mañana**, **Ayer por ayer**) creo en el amor.

¡Se llevan como perro y gato!

(trans.): **They fight like cats and dogs!**
(lit.): **They fight like dog and cat!**

¡Se llevan como perro y gato!

Paulina: Estaba pensando **para mis adentros** que lo mejor hubiera sido pedirle a mis huéspedes que se fueran **en el acto** pero lo que pasa es que soy muy **blanda de corazón**.Te digo que la verdad es que la situación va **de mal en peor**. Se me **pega como una ladilla**. No solo eso sino que ayer estaba limpiando mi florero favorito y lo **hizo añicos**. Y además **come como un desfondado**. Yo iba a **pasar por alto** algunas de las cosas que hace, pero francamente, ¡no le soporto ni un instante más!

Elena: Pero, solo es por un par de semanas.

Paulina: Ya lo sé, pero me está **volviendo loca** y anda **como Pedro por su casa**. Te digo que estoy **a dos dedos** de gritar. ¡Tengo ganas de **romperle la crisma**! **No es cosa de juego**. ¡Tengo **los nervios de punta**!

Elena: No quiero **meter las narices en** lo que no me importa, pero se ve **a todas luces**, le tienes que pedir que se vaya. Va a ser **pan comido**.

Paulina: Tienes razón. La verdad es que **nos llevamos como perro y gato**. Además yo tengo que **mirar por mis intereses** sin **partirle el corazón**. Yo siempre **me las he arreglado** sola y nunca he tenido estos problemas.

Lesson Six

Paulina: I was **thinking to myself** that maybe the best thing would be to just ask him to leave **right away** but I'm just too **soft-hearted**. I'm telling you, the situation **is going from bad to worse**. He **sticks to me like glue**. Not only that, but yesterday he was cleaning my favorite vase and **smashed it to smithereens**. And he **eats like a pig**. I was willing to **overlook** some of the things he did, but frankly, I don't think I can **put up with** him any longer!

Elena: But it's only for two weeks.

Paulina: I know, but he's already **driving me crazy** and he **acts like he owns the place**. I'm telling you, I'm **on the verge of** screaming. I feel like **ringing his neck**! **It's no laughing matter**. My **nerves are on edge**!

Elena: I don't want to **stick my nose in** other people's business, but **no matter how you look at it**, you just have to ask him to leave. It'll be **a cinch**.

Paulina: You're right. The truth is that we always **fight like cats and dogs**. Besides, I've got to **look out for number one** without **breaking his heart**. I've always **managed** things by myself and I've never had these kinds of problems before.

They fight like dog and cat!

Paulina: I was **thinking by my insides** that maybe the best thing would be to just ask him to leave **in the act** but I'm just too **soft of heart**. I'm telling you, the situation **is going from bad to worse**. He **sticks to me like a crab louse**. Not only that, but yesterday he was cleaning my favorite vase and **made it into fragments**. And he **eats like someone without a bottom**. I was willing to **overlook** some of the things he did but frankly, I don't think I can put up with him any longer!

Elena: But it's only for two weeks.

Paulina: I know, but he's already **turning me crazy** and he **acts like Pedro in his house**. I'm telling you, I'm **two fingers away from** screaming. I feel like **breaking his chrism**! **It's not a thing of game**. My **nerves are on end**!

Elena: I don't want to **put the nose into** other people's business, but **by all lights**, you just have to ask him to leave. It'll be **eaten bread**.

Paulina: You're right. The truth is that we always **fight like dog and cat**. Besides, I've got to **look out for my interests** without **breaking his heart**. I've always managed things by myself and I've never had these kinds of problems before.

Vocabulary

a dos dedos de (estar) *exp.* to be on the verge of • (lit.): to be two fingers from.

> *example:* Estoy **a dos dedos de** comprar una casa.
>
> *translation:* I'm **on the verge of** buying a house.
>
> **ALSO:** **dedo** *m.* a little bit • (lit.): finger • *beber un dedo de vino;* to drink a drop of wine.

a todas luces *exp.* any way you look at it, clearly • (lit.): by all lights.

> *example:* Se ve que tiene dinero **a todas luces**.
>
> *translation:* You can **clearly** tell he's got money.
>
> **SYNONYM:** **a toda luz** *exp.* • (lit.): by all light.
>
> **ALSO:** **de pocas luces** *exp.* stupid, dim-witted • (lit.): of little lights.
>
> > **NOTE:** This could best be compared to the American expression, "the lights are on but nobody's home."

arreglárselas para *exp.* to manage to • (lit.): to arrange oneself by.

> *example:* No puedo **arreglármelas para** levantar esta caja. ¿Me puedes ayudar?
>
> *translation:* I can't **manage to** lift this heavy box. Can you help me?
>
> **ALSO:** **¡Ya te arreglaré!** *exp.* I'll fix you!, I'll get even with you! • (lit.): I'll arrange you!

blando/a de corazón (ser) *exp.* to be soft-hearted • (lit.): to be soft of heart.

> *example:*   Marcos es muy **blando de corazón**.

> *translation:*   Marcos is very **soft-hearted**.

> **ANTONYM -1:**   **corazón de piedra (tener)** *exp.* to be very hard-hearted • (lit.): to have a heart made of stone.

> **ANTONYM -2:**   **duro/a de corazón (ser)** *exp.* to be hard-hearted • (lit.): to be hard of heart.

comer como un desfondado *exp.* to eat like a pig • (lit.): to eat like someone without a bottom (to eat like a bottomless pit).

> *example:*   Jorge está tan gordo porque siempre **come como un desfondado**.

> *translation:*   Jorge is so fat because he always **eats like a pig**.

> **SYNONYM -1:**   **comer como si fuera la última cena** *exp.* • (lit.): to eat as if it were the last supper.

> **SYNONYM -2:**   **comer como si no hubiera comido nunca** *exp.* • (lit.): to eat as if one never ate before.

> **NOTE:**   The noun *desfondado* comes from the verb *desfondar* meaning "to go through" or "to break the bottom of."

como Pedro por su casa *exp.* to feel right at home, to act like one owns the place • (lit.): like Pedro in his house.

> *example:*   Juan siempre anda en la oficina **como Pedro por su casa**.

> *translation:*   Juan always walks around the office **as if he owned the place**.

de mal en peor (ir) *exp.* to go from bad to worse • (lit.): [same].

> *example:*   Las cosas van **de mal en peor** entre Fernando y Verónica.

> *translation:*   Things are going **from bad to worse** between Fernando and Veronica.

> **ALSO:**   **mal que bien** *exp.* one way or another • (lit.): bad than good.

en el acto *exp.* • **1.** right away, immediately • **2.** in the act [of doing something] • (lit.): in the act.

> *example:* Voy a hacer la tarea **en el acto**.
>
> *translation:* I'm going to do my homework **right away**.
>
> **SYNONYM -1:** **acto continuo/seguido** *exp.* same as definition **1** above • (lit.): continuous/ consecutive act.
>
> **SYNONYM -2:** **ahora mismo** *exp.* same as **1** and **2** above • (lit.): now the same.
>
> **SYNONYM -3:** **de inmediato** *exp.* same as definition **1** above • (lit.): of immediate.

hacer añicos *exp.* • **1.** (of objects) to smash to smithereens • **2.** (of paper) to rip to shreds • (lit.): to make (into) fragments or bits.

> *example:* Elena **hizo añicos** mi plato favorito.
>
> *translation:* Elena **smashed** my favorite plate **to smithereens**.
>
> **SYNONYM:** **hacer pedazitos** *exp.* • (lit.): to make little pieces.
>
> **ALSO:** **estar hecho/a añicos** *exp.* to be worn out, exhausted • (lit.): to be made into fragments or bits.

llevarse como perro y gato *exp.* not to get along, to fight like cats and dogs • (lit.): to carry each other like dog and cat.

> *example:* Teresa y Carlos **se llevan como perro y gato**.
>
> *translation:* Teresa and Carlos **fight like cats and dogs**.
>
> **NOTE:** Make sure to be aware of the difference between the Spanish expression and its English equivalent. In the Spanish expression, it's *perro y gato*; "dog and cat," both singular. However, in English the order is opposite; "cats and dogs," both plural.
>
> **SYNONYM -1:** **llevarse mal con** *exp.* • (lit.): to carry oneself off badly with.
>
> **SYNONYM -2:** **no hacer buenas migas con** *exp.* • (lit.): not to make good bread crumbs with.
>
> **ANTONYM -1:** **llevarse bien con** *exp.* to get along well with • (lit.): to carry oneself off well with.
>
> **ANTONYM -2:** **hacer buenas migas con** *exp.* to get along well with • (lit.): to make good bread crumbs with.

meter las narices en lo que a uno no le importa *exp.* to

butt into other people's business, to stick one's nose into everything •
(lit.): to put the nose into that which doesn't concern one.

> *example:* Darío siempre **mete las narices donde no le importa**.
>
> *translation:* Dario always **sticks his nose into everything**.
>
> **ALSO -1:** **en sus mismas narices** *exp.* right under one's nose • (lit.): in one's own nose.
>
> **ALSO -2:** **hablar por las narices** *exp.* to talk through one's nose • (lit.): to talk through one's nose.
>
> **ALSO -3:** **tener algo delante de las narices** *exp.* to have something right under one's nose • (lit.): to have something right in front of one's nose.

mirar por sus [proprios] intereses *exp.* to look out for oneself,

to look out for number one • (lit.): to look out for one's [own] interests.

> *example:* A Simón no le importa la gente. Solo **mira por sus [propios] intereses**.
>
> *translation:* Simón doesn't care about other people. He only **looks out for number one**.
>
> **SYNONYM:** **preocuparse solo de uno mismo** *exp.* to worry only about oneself • (lit.): [same].

nervios de punta (tener los) *exp.* to be edgy, to be very nervous

• (lit.): to have one's nerves on end.

> *example:* ¡**Tengo los nervios de punta**!
>
> *translation:* **I'm so edgy**!
>
> **SYNONYM:** **estar hecho un manojo de nervios** *exp.* to be a bundle of nerves • (lit.): to be made a bundle of nerves.

no ser cosa de juego *exp.* to be no laughing matter • (lit.): not to be a

thing of game.

> *example:* ¡Esto **no es cosa de juego**!
>
> *translation:* This **is no laughing matter**!

> **ALSO -1:** **hacer doble juego** *exp.* to be two-faced • (lit.): to make double game.
>
> **ALSO -2:** **hacer juego** *exp.* to match, to go well with (as in clothes) • (lit.): to make game.
>
> **ALSO -3:** **prestarse al juego** *exp.* to go along with the game • (lit.): to borrow the game.

pan comido (ser) *exp.* to be easy, a cinch • (lit.): to be eaten bread.

> *example:* Este examen es **pan comido**.
>
> *translation:* This test is **a cinch**.
>
> **SYNONYM:** **estar tirado/a** *adj. (Spain)* • (lit.): to be thrown away • *Este examen está tirado;* This test is so easy.

partirle el corazón a alguien *exp.* to break someone's heart • (lit.): to break someone's heart.

> *example:* Parece que Laura **le rompió el corazón a Felipe**.
>
> *translation:* It looks like Laura **broke Felipe's heart**.

pasar por alto *exp.* to overlook • (lit.): to overpass.

> *example:* Yo iba a **pasar por alto** algunas cosas, pero esto es demasiado.
>
> *translation:* I was going **to overlook** some things, but this is too much.

pegarse como una ladilla *exp.* to stick to someone like glue • (lit.): to stick to someone like a crab (as in pubic lice).

> *example:* Alberto es un pesado. Siempre **se pega como una ladilla**.
>
> *translation:* Alberto is a pain. He **sticks to me like glue**.
>
> **NOTE:** This expression is considered somewhat crude and should be used with discretion.
>
> **ALSO:** **pegarle cuatro gritos a alguien** *exp.* to give someone a piece of one's mind, to rake someone over the coals • (lit.): to let out four screams to someone.

pensar para sus adentros *exp.* to think to oneself • (lit.): to think by one's insides.

> *example:*   Estaba yo **pensando para mis adentros** que sería bueno hacer un viaje a Paris este verano.

> *translation:*   I was **thinking to myself** that it would be nice to go on a trip to Paris next summer.

romper la crisma a alguien *exp.* to ring someone's neck. • (lit.): to break someone's chrism.

> *example:*   Como no te portes bien, **te voy a romper la crisma**.

> *translation:*   If you don't behave well, I'm **going to ring your neck**.

> **SYNONYM -1:**   **romperle el alma a alguien** *exp.* • (lit.): to break someone's soul.

> **SYNONYM -2:**   **romperle el bautismo a alguien** *exp.* • (lit.): to break one's baptism.

> **SYNONYM -3:**   **romperle la cara a alguien** *exp.* to smash someone's face • (lit.): [same].

> **SYNONYM -4:**   **romperle la nariz [a alguien]** *exp.* • (lit.): to break someone's nose.

volver loco/a a uno/a *exp.* to drive someone crazy • (lit.): to turn someone crazy.

> *example:*   ¡Me estás **volviendo loco**!

> *translation:*   You're **driving me crazy**!

> **ALSO -1:**   **cada loco con su tema** *exp.* everyone does his own thing • (lit.): each crazy person with his/her own theme.

> **ALSO -2:**   **suerte loca** *exp.* unbelievably good luck • (lit.): crazy luck.

> **ALSO -3:**   **volverse loco/a** *exp.* to go crazy • (lit.): to turn crazy.

Practice the Vocabulary

(Answers to Lesson Six, p. 200)

A. Complete the following phrases by choosing the appropriate word(s) from the list below.

a todas luces   meter las narices
como perro y gato   no es cosa de juego
de mal en peor   Pedro por su casa
en el acto   pensé para mis adentros
hizo añicos   romperle la crisma
los nervios de punta   volver loca

1. Carlos es una cotilla; le gusta _____ en los asuntos de los demás.

2. Si escucho esta canción una sola vez más, me voy a _____.

3. La última vez que estuvo en mi casa, _____ mi jarrón favorito.

4. _____ que no pueda parar de estornudar cada vez que salgo a la calle en primavera.

5. Se ve _____ que le gustas mucho.

6. La situación en mi trabajo va _____; estoy deseando irme de allí.

7. Cada vez que viajo en avión se me ponen _____.

8. Le reconoció _____, aunque hacía veinte años que no le veía.

9. Cuando vino a mi oficina, estaba tan cómodo que iba como _____.

10. El otro día _____ lo mucho que me apetece irme de vacaciones.

11. Javier y su hermano se llevan _____. Siempre se están peleando.

12. No le aguanto más. Tengo ganas de _____.

B. Underline the appropriate word(s) that best complete(s) the phrase.

1. Nunca puedo decir que no; soy demasiado (**corazonado**, **corazones blandos**, **blando de corazón**).

2. El día de Navidad todo el mundo come (**con un desconocido**, **como desfondados**, **sin desfondar**).

3. Aunque hacía mucho frío, el otro día (**estuve a dos dedos**, **estuve con dos dedos**, **tenía dos dedos**) de bañarme en el mar.

4. Miriam es una persona muy sensible. Con cualquier cosa que le dices se (**parten las manos**, **corazón roto**, **le parte el corazón**).

5. Tengo que (**mirar más a menudo**, **mirar por mis intereses**, **interesarme en mirar**); voy a mudarme a una casa más barata.

6. Su matrimonio (**va de mal en peor**, **mal y peor**, **va y viene**). Yo creo que van a divorciarse.

7. Para Michael Jordan meter una canasta es (**pan comido**, **comer pan**, **un trozo de tarta**).

8. Pablo se (**está pegando a una ladilla**, **marea mucho**, **pega como una ladilla**); no puede estar solo.

9. Este año (**una casa nueva**, **el sol brillará**, **me las he arreglado**) para conseguir una semana más de vacaciones.

10. Juan y Pedro (**se llevan como perro y gato**, **tienen perros y gatos**, **se llevaron al gato**); no pueden estar juntos.

11. Cuando hay mucho trabajo (**hay puntas**, **tengo puntas en los nervios**, **tengo los nervios de punta**).

12. No me gusta (**meter las narices**, **estar con narices**, **las narices**) en los problemas de los demás.

C. Match the English phrase in the left column with the Spanish translation from the right. Mark the appropriate letter in the box.

☐ 1. Last time I moved, all my china was smashed to smithereens.

☐ 2. If he doesn't leave right now, he is going to drive me crazy.

☐ 3. Ernesto doesn't care about other people. He only looks out for himself.

☐ 4. No matter how you look at it, it's going to take you a long time to finish this work.

☐ 5. Eduardo sticks to Susana like glue.

☐ 6. I was on the verge of asking him to leave my house.

☐ 7. He likes to help people out. He is very soft-hearted.

☐ 8. He discovered right away that she was lying to him.

☐ 9. I am thinking to myself that I should tell her what I really feel.

☐ 10. Jorge broke my heart when he told me he was moving away.

☐ 11. Crime in this country is no laughing matter.

☐ 12. David eats like a pig when he is really hungry.

A. Juan **me partió el corazón** cuando me dijo que se iba a vivir a otro lugar.

B. Estuve **a dos dedos de** echarle de mi casa.

C. David **come como un desfondado** cuando tiene mucha hambre.

D. Estoy **pensando para mis adentros** que debería decirle lo que realmente siento.

E. Él siempre ayuda a los demás, es muy **bueno de corazón**.

F. La delincuencia en este país **no es cosa de juego**.

G. Eduardo siempre va **pegado como una ladilla** a Susana.

H. A Ernesto no le importa la gente. Solo **mira por sus propios intereses**.

I. En la última mudanza, toda la vajilla **se hizo añicos**.

J. Descubrió **en el acto** que ella le estaba mintiendo.

K. Se nota **a todas luces** que no te gusta el repollo, así que no te los comas.

L. Como no se vaya de una vez, **me voy a volver loca**.

D. CROSSWORD
Fill in the crossword puzzle on page 112 by choosing the correct word(s) from the list below.

acto	gato	narices
adentros	intereses	pan
corazón	juego	Pedro
crisma	ladilla	peor
dedos	loco	punta
desfondado	luces	

ACROSS

10. **pegarse como una** _____ *exp.* to stick to someone like glue • (lit.): to stick to someone like a crab (as in pubic lice).

14. **nervios de** _____ **(tener los)** *exp.* to be edgy, to be very nervous • (lit.): to have one's nerves on end.

18. **a todas** _____ *exp.* any way you look at it, clearly • (lit.): by all lights.

26. **como** _____ **por su casa** *exp.* to feel right at home • (lit.): like Pedro in his house.

31. **comer como un** _____ *exp.* to eat like a pig • (lit.): to eat as if one's botton fell off.

37. **de mal en** _____ **(ir)** *exp.* to go from bad to worse • (lit.): [same].

45. **volver** _____ **a uno/a** *exp.* to drive someone crazy • (lit.): to turn someone crazy.

51. **romper la _____ a alguien** *exp.* to ring someone's neck. •
    (lit.): to break one's chrism.

56. **a dos _____ de (estar)** *exp.* to be on the verge of • (lit.): to be
    two fingers from.

DOWN

2. **_____ comido (ser)** *exp.* to be easy, a cinch • (lit.): to be eaten
   bread.

11. **mirar por sus _____** *exp.* to look out for oneself, to look out for
    number one • (lit.): to look out for one's interests.

15. **pensar para sus _____** *exp.* to think to oneself • (lit.): to think
    by one's insides.

20. **no ser cosa de _____** *exp.* to be no laughing matter • (lit.): not
    to be a thing of game.

24. **blando/a de _____ (ser)** *exp.* to be soft-hearted • (lit.): to be
    soft of heart.

32. **meter las _____ en lo que a uno no le importa** *exp.* to
    butt into other people's business, to stick one's nose into every-
    thing • (lit.): to put the nose into that which doesn't concern one.

48. **en el _____** *exp.* • **1.** right the way, immediately, on the spot •
    2. in the act [of doing something] • (lit.): in the act.

49. **llevarse como perro y _____** *exp.* not to get along, to fight
    like cats and dogs • (lit.): to carry each other like dog and cat.

CROSSWORD PUZZLE

E. DICTATION
Test Your Aural Comprehension

(This dictation can be found in the Appendix on page 211.)

If you are following along with your cassette, you will now hear a series of sentences from the opening dialogue. These sentences will be read by a native speaker at normal conversational speed (which may seem fast to you at first). In addition, the words will be pronounced as you would actually hear them in a conversation, often including some common reductions.

The first time the sentences are presented, simply listen in order to get accustomed to the speed and heavy use of reductions. The sentences will then be read again with a pause after each to give you time to write down what you heard. The third time the sentences are read, follow along with what you have written.

Hoy, tengo los huesos molidos.

(trans.): **I'm wiped out today**.
(lit.): **I have ground up bones today**.

Hoy, tengo los huesos molidos

Ignacio: Tengo una idea. Me estoy **muriendo de ganas** de ir a un picnic hoy y hay un parque **a dos pasos de aquí**. Podemos almorzar allí y luego **dar una vuelta** por el parque.

Teresa: ¡**Trato hecho**! Me encantaría **tomar un poco de aire fresco**. Y **de todas maneras**, será divertido **clavarle los ojos** a toda la gente. ¡Vamos!

Ignacio: ¡Qué raro! ¡**No hay ni cuatro gatos** aquí! Nunca se me olvidará lo que me pasó aquí la última vez. Yo **tenía los huesos molidos** y me **dormí a fondo boca abajo**. Cuando me desperté, me di cuenta que había estado **lloviendo a cántaros** por mucho tiempo...**cosa de** una hora. ¡Qué **tiempo de perros**! ¡**Estaba hecho una sopa**! ¡Tenía tanto frío que hasta se **me puso la carne de gallina**!

Teresa: Yo siempre llevo un paraguas conmigo **por si acaso**. **Más vale prevenir que curar**. ¿Sabes? La última vez que estuve aquí **vi por el rabo del ojo** a un hombre **corriendo a toda prisa**. ¡Luego me di cuenta de que estaba **en cueros**! ¡**Se me pusieron los pelos de punta**!

Ignacio: Ese hombre debe haber estado **loco de remate**. ¡Me imagino que **hizo furor con** las mujeres!

Ignacio: I have an idea. I'm **dying to** to go on a picnic today and there's a park that's **a hop, skip, and a jump from here**. We can have lunch and then **take a stroll** through the park.

Teresa: **It's a deal**! It'll be nice to **get a breath of fresh air**. And **at any rate**, it'll be fun to **check out** all the people. Let's go!

Ignacio: How strange! **There's hardly a soul here**! I'll never forget what happen to me last time I was here. I was **wiped out** and I **fell fast asleep on my stomach**. When I woke up, I realized that it'd been **raining cats and dogs** for a long time... **approximately** one hour. What **lousy weather**! I was **soaked**! I was so cold I got **goose bumps**!

Teresa: I always bring an umbrella with me wherever I go **just in case**. **Better safe than sorry**. You know, the last time I was here, I looked out of the **corner of my eye** and saw a guy running **at full speed**. Then I noticed he was **stark-naked**! **My hair stood on end**!

Ignacio: The guy must have been **nuts**. I imagine he was **quite a hit with** the women!

I have ground up bones today

Ignacio: I have an idea. I'm **dying of wish** to go on a picnic today and there's a park that's **two steps from here**. We can have lunch and then **give a turn** through the park.

Teresa: **Deal done**! It'll be nice to **take a little of the fresh air**. And **at any rate** it'll be fun to **nail our eyes on** all the people. Let's go!

Ignacio: How strange! **There aren't even four cats here**! I'll never forget what happen to me last time I was here. I **had ground up bones** and I **fell asleep with the mouth under**. When I woke up, I realized that it'd been **raining pitcherfuls** for a long time... **thing of** one hour. What **weather of dogs**! I was **made into a soup**! I was so cold I got **chicken meat**!

Teresa: I always bring an umbrella with me wherever I go **by if case**. **It's worth more to prevent than to cure**. You know, the last time I was here, I looked out of the **tail of the eye** and saw a guy running **at all speed**. Then I noticed he was **in his own hide**! **It put my hair on end**!

Ignacio: The guy must have been **crazy of end**. I imagine he was **making fury with** the women!

Vocabulary

a dos pasos de aquí *exp.* nearby, a hop, skip, and a jump from here • (lit.): two steps from here.

> *example:*   La casa de Laura está **a dos pasos de** aquí.
>
> *translation:*   Laura's house is **a hop, skip, and a jump** from here.
>
> **ANTONYM:**   **en el quinto pino** *exp.* very far away • (lit.): in the fifth pine tree.

a toda prisa *exp.* at full speed, as quickly as possible • (lit.): at all speed.

> *example:*   Salí de mi casa **a toda prisa** cuando me enteré de la emergencia.
>
> *translation:*   I left my house **as quickly as possible** when I heard about the emergency.
>
> **SYNONYM -1:**   **a toda vela** *exp.* • (lit.): at all sail.
>
> **SYNONYM -2:**   **en menos que canta un gallo** *exp.* • (lit.): in less time than a hen can sing.
>
> **SYNONYM -3:**   **en un avemaría** *exp.* • (lit.): in one Hail Mary.
>
> **SYNONYM -4:**   **en un periquete** *exp.* (Southern Spain).

carne de gallina *exp.* goose bumps • (lit.): chicken meat.

> *example:*   Se me puso **la carne de gallina** cuando oí las noticias.
>
> *translation:*   I got **goose bumps** when I heard the news.
>
> **ALSO -1:**   **gallina** *m. & f.* coward, "chicken" • (lit.): chicken.
>
> **ALSO -2:**   **ponérsele a uno la carne de gallina** *exp.* to get goose bumps • (lit.): to have one's flesh turn into that of a hen.

clavar los ojos a/en *exp.* to stare at, to fix one's eyes on, to check out • (lit.): to nail one's eyes on.

> *example:*   No puedo dejar de **clavarle los ojos a** este cuadro. ¡Es precioso!

> *translation:*   I can't stop **staring at** that painting. It's beautiful!

> **SYNONYM -1:**   **clavar la atención en** *exp.* • (lit.): to fix one's attention on.

> **SYNONYM -2:**   **clavar la vista en** *exp.* • (lit.): to nail the sight on.

> **SYNONYM -3:**   **hacer ojitos** *exp. (Mexico & some regions of Spain)* • (lit.): to make little eyes.

> **SYNONYM -4:**   **hacer ojos** *exp. (Colombia)* • (lit.): to make eyes.

> **ALSO -1:**   **guiñar un ojo** *exp.* to make eyes at, to flirt • (lit.): to wink an eye.

> **ALSO -2:**   **hacer caras** *exp. (Eastern Argentina, Uruguay)* to make eyes at, to flirt • (lit.): to make faces.

cosa de *exp.* approximately, about, more or less • (lit.): thing of.

> *example:*   Vuelvo en **cosa de** dos horas.

> *translation:*   I'll be back **in approximately** two hours.

> **NOTE:**   **ser cosas de...** *exp.* to be the way ... is • (lit.): to be things of • *Esas son cosas de Javier;* That's just the way Javier is.

> **ALSO:**   **cosa de ver** *exp.* something to see • (lit.): [same].

dar una vuelta *exp.* to take a stroll, a walk • (lit.): to give a turn.

> *example:*   Hace un día muy bonito. Vamos a **dar una vuelta**.

> *translation:*   It's a beautiful day. Let's **go for a stroll**.

> **SYNONYM -1:**   **dar un paseo** *exp.* • (lit.): to give a passage.

> **SYNONYM -2:**   **pasear a pie** *exp.* • (lit.): to walk by foot.

> **SYNONYM -3:**   **tomar el aire** *exp.* • (lit.): to take the air.

de todas maneras *exp.* at any rate, in any case • (lit.): in all manners.

> *example:* No puedo creerme cuánto trabajo tengo. **De todas maneras**, me voy a Inglaterra por la mañana.

> *translation:* I can't believe how much work I have to do. **At any rate**, I'm leaving for England in the morning.

> **SYNONYM:** **de todos modos** *exp.* • (lit.): in all modes.

dormir [a fondo] boca abajo *exp.* to sleep on one's stomach • (lit.): to sleep [deeply] with the mouth under.

> *example:* Desde que Estefanía se dañó la espalda, solo puede **dormir a fondo boca abajo**.

> *translation:* Ever since Estefanía hurt her back, she can only **sleep on her stomach**.

> **SYNONYM:** **dormir a pata suelta** *exp.* • (lit.): to sleep with a lose leg.

en cueros (estar) *exp.* naked, in one's birthday suit • (lit.): in one's own hide.

> *example:* Ese bebé debe tener mucho frío porque **está en cueros**.

> *translation:* That baby must be very cold because he is **completely naked**.

> **SYNONYM -1:** **en cueros vivos** *exp.* • (lit.): in one's own living hide.
> **SYNONYM -2:** **en pelotas** *exp.* *(Spain)* • (lit.): in balls.
> **SYNONYM -3:** **en el traje de Adán** *exp.* • (lit.): in the suit of Adam.
> **SYNONYM -4:** **encuerado/a** *adj.* • (lit.): skinned.
> **SYNONYM -5:** **en pila** *f.* *(Ecuador, Peru, Bolivia)* • (lit.): heap, pile.

estar hecho una sopa *exp.* to be drenched, soaking wet • (lit.): to be made into a soup.

> *example:* Susana llegó al trabajo **hecha una sopa**.

> *translation:* Susana was **soaking wet** by the time she got to work.

SYNONYM: **estar empapado/a** *adj.* • (lit.): to be soaking wet.

ALSO: **comer de la sopa boba** *exp.* to live off others • (lit.): to eat from the stupid soup.

> **NOTE:** *Sopa boba* is a type of soup similar to French onion soup.

hacer un gran furor *exp.* to be a big event, to make a big splash • (lit.): to make fury.

example: ¡Oí que **hiciste un gran furor** con el jefe!

translation: I heard you **made a big splash** with the boss!

SYNONYM: **tener un éxito padre** *exp.* *(Mexico)* to have a father success.

llover a cántaros *exp.* to rain cats and dogs • (lit.): to rain pitcherfuls.

example: No podemos ir al parque porque está **lloviendo a cántaros**.

translation: We can't go to the park because **it's raining cats and dogs**.

SYNONYM -1: **caer burros aparejados** *exp.* *(Cuba, Puerto Rico, Dominican Republic)* • (lit.): to fall prepared donkeys.

SYNONYM -2: **caer el diluvio** *exp.* • (lit.): to fall the Flood (as in the Bible).

SYNONYM -3: **caer un chaparrón** *exp.* • (lit.): to fall a downpour.

SYNONYM -4: **llover a chorros** *exp.* • (lit.): to rain in spurts.

SYNONYM -5: **llover con rabia** *exp.* *(Cuba, Puerto Rico, Dominican Republic, Southern Spain)* • (lit.): to rain with anger (or fury).

ALSO: **mucho ha llovido desde entonces** *exp.* a lot of water has flowed under the bridge since then • (lit.): a lot has rained since then.

loco/a de remate (estar) *exp.* to be totally crazy, nuts, hopelessly mad • (lit.): crazy of end.

example: Eduardo está **loco de remate**. Siempre habla consigo mismo en público.

translation: Eduardo is **totally crazy**. He always talks to himself in public.

SYNONYM -1: **como una cabra (estar)** *exp.* • (lit.): to be like a goat.

SYNONYM -2: **loco/a de atar (estar)** *exp.* • (lit.): to be crazy to restrict.

más vale prevenir que curar *exp.* better to be safe than sorry • (lit.): it's worth more to prevent than to cure.

example: **Más vale prevenir que curar**. Voy a traer el paraguas por si llueve.

translation: **Better safe than sorry**. I'm going to bring my umbrella just in case it rains.

morir de ganas *exp.* to be dying to do something, to feel like • (lit.): to die of wish.

example: **Me muero de ganas** por ver a María.

translation: **I'm dying** to see Maria.

SYNONYM: **tener muchas ganas de** *exp.* • (lit.): to have many desires to.

ALSO -1: **morirse de aburrimiento** *exp.* to be bored to death, bored stiff • (lit.): to die of boredom.

ALSO -2: **morirse de frío** *exp.* to be very cold, to be freezing • (lit.): to die of cold.

ALSO -3: **morirse de hambre** *exp.* to be very hungry • (lit.): to starve to death.

ALSO -4: **morirse de risa** *exp.* to die laughing • (lit.): to die laughing.

ALSO -5: **morirse de sed** *exp.* to be dying of thirst • (lit.): to die of thirst.

no hay ni cuatro gatos *exp.* there's hardly a soul • (lit.): not to be even four cats.

example: En esta fiesta **no hay ni cuatro gatos**.

translation: There's **hardly a soul** at this party.

ANTONYM -1:	**estar de bote en bote** *exp.* to be very crowded • (lit.): to be from boat to boat.
ANTONYM -2:	**estar hasta los botes** *exp.* to be very crowed • (lit.): to be up to the boats.

ponerse los pelos de punta *exp.* to have one's hair stand on end • (lit.): to put one's hairs on end.

> *example:* **Se me pusieron los pelos de punta** cuando vi al elefante escaparse del zoológico.
>
> *translation:* **My hair stood on end** when I saw the elephant escaping from the zoo.

ALSO -1:	**cortar/partir un cabello en el aire** *exp.* to split hairs • (lit.): to cut/to split a hair in the air.
ALSO -2:	**no tener un pelo de tonto** *exp.* to be nobody's fool • (lit.): not to have a hair of a fool.
ALSO -3:	**por los pelos** *exp.* by the skin of one's teeth • (lit.): by the hairs.

por si acaso *exp.* just in case • (lit.): by if case.

> *example:* Voy a llevar mi abrigo **por si acaso** hace frío más tarde.
>
> *translation:* I'm going to bring my coat with me **just in case** it gets colder later.

rabo del ojo (mirar/ver por el) *exp.* to look/to see out of the corner of the eye • (lit.): to look/to see by the tail of the eye.

> *example:* **Miré con el rabo del ojo** y vi que todo el mundo se estaba fijando en mí.
>
> *translation:* **I looked out of the corner of my eye** and I saw that everybody was staring at me.

SYNONYM:	**mirar/ver de reojo** *exp.* • (lit.): to look suspiciously at.
ALSO:	**con el rabo entre las piernas** *exp.* with one's tail between one's legs • (lit.): [same].

tener los huesos molidos *exp.* to be wiped out, exhausted, ready to collapse • (lit.): to have ground up bones.

> *example:* He trabajado todo el día. **Tengo los huesos molidos**.
>
> *translation:* I've worked all day long. **I'm wiped out**.
>
> **SYNONYM -1:** **estar hecho/a polvo** *exp.* *(Spain)* • (lit.): to be made of dust.
>
> **SYNONYM -2:** **estar hecho/a un trapo** *exp.* to be made of rag.
>
> **SYNONYM -3:** **estar reventado/a** *adj.* • (lit.): to be smashed.

tiempo de perros *exp.* lousy weather • (lit.): weather of dogs.

> *example:* Hoy hace un **tiempo de perros**.
>
> *translation:* Today we're having **lousy weather**.
>
> **ALSO -1:** **vida de perro** *exp.* a hard life • (lit.): a dog's life.
>
> **ALSO -2:** **ponerle al mal tiempo buena cara** *exp.* to make the best of things • (lit.): to put a good face to the bad weather.

tomar un poco de aire fresco *exp.* to get some fresh air • (lit.): to take a little fresh air.

> *example:* Me duele la cabeza. Voy a **tomar un poco de aire fresco**.
>
> *translation:* I have a headache. I'm going **to get some fresh air**.
>
> **SYNONYM:** **tomar el fresco** *exp.* • (lit.): to take some fresh (air).
>
> **ALSO -1:** **ponerse fresco** *exp.* to put on light clothing (for the summer, etc) • (lit.): to put oneself fresh.
>
> **ALSO -2:** **tomar el aire** *exp.* to take a walk • (lit.): to take air.

trato hecho *exp.* it's a deal • (lit.): deal done.

> *example:* **Trato hecho**. Te compro la motocicleta.
>
> *translation:* **It's a deal**. I'll buy your motorcycle.

Practice the Vocabulary

(Answers to Lesson Seven, p. 201)

A. Underline the correct definition of the slang word(s) in boldface.

1. **más vale prevenir que curar**:
   a. easier said than done
   b. better to be safe than sorry

2. **a dos pasos de aquí**:
   a. very far away
   b. just around the corner

3. **de todas maneras**:
   a. at any rate
   b. no way

4. **loco de remate**:
   a. crazy
   b. sane

5. **no hay ni cuatro gatos**:
   a. there are too many people
   b. there is hardly a soul

6. **se me pusieron los pelos de punta**:
   a. I got chills
   b. my hair stood on end

7. **tener los huesos molidos**:
   a. to be wiped out
   b. to be in good shape

8. **estar en cueros**:
   a. to be all dressed up
   b. to be stark-naked

9. **cosa de**:
   a. approximately
   b. exactly

10. **mirar por el rabo del ojo**:
    a. to stare at
    b. to look out of the corner of the eye

11. **estar hecho una sopa**:
    a. to be soaked
    b. to be dry

12. **tiempo de perros**:
    a. good weather
    b. lousy weather

B. Complete the phrase by filling in the blank with the appropriate word(s) from the list below. Make all necessary changes.

a dar una vuelta	**lloviendo a cántaros**
a toda prisa	**loco de remate**
a dos pasos de aquí	**los huesos molidos**
había ni cuatro gatos	**más vale prevenir que curar**
hizo furor	**muero de ganas**
la carne de gallina	**trato hecho**

1. Ernesto vive cerquísima, sólo _____.

2. Siempre tengo _____ después de jugar al fútbol.

3. _____, me voy contigo a cenar después del trabajo.

4. Vi a un hombre corriendo _____ y me asusté.

5. Pedro está _____; hace unas cosas muy raras.

6. Tómate las medicinas, _____.

7. Me _____ por comerme un helado.

8. Hacía tanto frío que se me puso _____.

9. Ha estado _____ toda la noche; todo está mojado.

10. No _____ en el bar donde estuvimos anoche.

11. Estoy seguro de que Marta _____ con los chicos en la fiesta.

12. Me apetece ir a _____ por el parque.

C. Match the English phrase in the left column with the Spanish translation from the right. Mark the appropriate letter in the box.

☐ 1. Juan got so excited that he got goose bumps.

☐ 2. Teresa loves observing people.

☐ 3. The weather has been lousy lately.

☐ 4. I am dying to see Sharon Stone's latest movie.

☐ 5. Pablo is always in a hurry.

☐ 6. I'd love to take a stroll.

☐ 7. In spring it always rains cats and dogs.

☐ 8. Ignacio always carries his day-timer with him just in case.

☐ 9. Alfonso is quite a hit with the women.

☐ 10. I am tired. I need to get a breath of fresh air.

☐ 11. I will be at your house in about an hour.

☐ 12. I was so tired that I fell asleep on my stomach.

A. **Me muero de ganas** por ver la última película de Sharon Stone.

B. Estoy cansado. Necesito **tomar un poco de aire fresco**.

C. En primavera siempre **llueve a cántaros**.

D. Ignacio siempre lleva su agenda **por si acaso**.

E. Llegaré a tu casa **en cosa de** una hora.

F. Estaba tan cansado que me **dormí a fondo boca abajo**.

G. Juan se emocionó tanto que hasta **se le puso la carne de gallina**.

H. A Teresa le gusta **clavarle los ojos a** todo el mundo.

I. Me gustaría ir a **dar una vuelta**.

J. Últimamente hace **un tiempo de perros**.

K. Pablo siempre va corriendo **a toda prisa**.

L. Alfonso **hace gran furor con** las mujeres.

D. FIND-A-WORD PUZZLE
Using the list below, circle the words in the grid on page 132 that are missing from the Spanish idiom. Words may be spelled up, down, or across.

abajo	**furor**	**pelos**
acaso	**gallina**	**perros**
cántaros	**ganas**	**prisa**
cosa	**hecho**	**remate**
cuatro	**huesos**	**sopa**
cueros	**maneras**	**vuelta**
curar	**ojos**	
fresco	**pasos**	

1. *example:* **Me muero de** _____ por ver a María.

   translation: **I'm dying** to see Maria.

2. *example:* La casa de Laura está **a dos** _____ **de** aquí.

   translation: Laura's house is **a hop, skip, and a jump** from here.

3. *example:* Hace un día muy bonito. Vamos a **dar una** _____.

   translation: It's a beautiful day. Let's **go for a stroll**.

4. *example:* **Trato** _____. Te compro la motocicleta.

   translation: **It's a deal**. I'll buy your motorcycle.

5. *example:* Me duele la cabeza. Voy a **tomar un poco de aire** _____.

   translation: I have a headache. I'm going **to get some fresh air**.

6. *example:*   No puedo creerme cuánto trabajo tengo. **De todas**
    _____, me voy a Inglaterra por la mañana.

    translation: I can't believe how much work I have to do. **At any rate**, I'm leaving for England in the morning.

7. *example:*   No puedo dejar de **clavarle los** _____ **a** este cuadro. ¡Es precioso!

    translation: I can't stop **staring at** that painting. It's beautiful!

8. *example:*   En esta fiesta **no hay ni** _____ gatos.

    translation: There's **hardly a soul** at this party.

9. *example:*   He trabajado todo el día. **Tengo los** _____ **molidos**.

    translation: I've worked all day long. **I'm wiped out**.

10. *example:*   Desde que Estefanía se dañó la espalda, solo puede **dormir a fondo boca** _____.

    translation: Ever since Estefanía hurt her back, she can only **sleep on her stomach**.

11. *example:*   No podemos ir al parque porque está **lloviendo a** _____.

    translation: We can't go to the park because **it's raining cats and dogs**.

12. *example:*   Vuelvo en _____ **de** dos horas.

    translation: I'll be back **in approximately** two hours.

13. *example:*   Hoy hace un **tiempo de** _____.

    translation: Today we're having **lousy weather**.

14. *example:* Por culpa de la lluvia, Susana llegó al trabajo **hecha una _____**.

    translation: Because of all the rain, Susana was **soaking wet** by the time she got to work.

15. *example:* Se me puso **la carne de _____** cuando oí las noticias.

    translation: I got **goose bumps** when I heard the news.

16. *example:* Voy a llevar mi abrigo **por si _____** hace frío más tarde.

    translation: I'm going to bring my coat with me **just in case** it gets colder later.

17. *example:* Voy a traer el paraguas por si llueve. **Más vale prevenir que _____**.

    translation: I'm going to bring my umbrella just in case it rains. **Better safe than sorry**.

18. *example:* Salí de mi casa **a toda _____** cuando me enteré de la emergencia.

    translation: I left my house **as quickly as possible** when I heard about the emergency.

19. *example:* Ese bebé debe tener mucho frío porque **está en _____**.

    translation: That baby must be very cold because he's **completely naked**.

20. *example:* **Se me pusieron los _____ de punta** cuando vi al elefante escaparse del zoológico.

    translation: **My hair stood on end** when I saw the elephant escaping from the zoo.

21.   *example:*   Eduardo está **loco de** _____.
      translation: Eduardo is **completely crazy**.

22.   *example:*   ¡Oí que **hiciste un gran** _____ con el jefe!
      translation: I heard you made a big splash with the boss!

FIND-A-WORD PUZZLE

```
H  E  C  H  O  F  E  L  M  P  G  W
P  A  S  O  S  U  H  U  E  S  O  S
M  B  C  U  E  R  O  S  O  C  Z  R
A  A  U  M  A  O  P  M  S  M  P  A
O  J  O  S  P  R  E  E  S  E  E  S
A  O  E  N  R  A  R  R  I  E  L  T
G  N  S  G  I  F  O  P  T  A  O  O
U  T  L  A  S  L  S  A  L  C  S  A
A  A  P  N  A  O  M  L  O  Á  T  N
S  O  C  A  M  E  S  I  L  N  G  V
S  G  U  S  R  E  E  M  E  T  F  U
H  A  E  L  A  S  M  M  O  A  O  E
I  L  C  O  C  O  S  A  O  R  N  L
C  L  T  A  A  U  P  N  S  O  D  T
O  I  I  U  S  U  E  E  E  S  O  A
C  N  R  A  O  P  R  R  G  A  S  R
B  A  A  Z  O  M  R  A  G  A  R  O
C  U  A  T  R  O  O  S  M  M  M  J
C  U  R  A  R  C  S  N  R  A  D  O
```

E. DICTATION
Test Your Aural Comprehension

(This dictation can be found in the Appendix on page 212.)

If you are following along with your cassette, you will now hear a series of sentences from the opening dialogue. These sentences will be read by a native speaker at normal conversational speed (which may seem fast to you at first). In addition, the words will be pronounced as you would actually hear them in a conversation, often including some common reductions.

The first time the sentences are presented, simply listen in order to get accustomed to the speed and heavy use of reductions. The sentences will then be read again with a pause after each to give you time to write down what you heard. The third time the sentences are read, follow along with what you have written.

¡Lo mandé a bañar!

(trans.): **I told him to go take a flying leap!**
(lit.): **I sent him to go take a bath!**

¡Lo mandé a bañar!

Liliana: Así que **ponme al día**. ¿Cómo fueron tus vacaciones con Ramón? ¡Me imagino que te lo pasaste muy bien!

Vivian: **Ni mucho menos**. Fue horrible **de cabo a rabo**. Estuve **a punto** de **hacer el equipaje** y volver a casa al siguiente día...o de **mandarlo a bañar**. ¡**No quiero tener nada que ver** con él otra vez!

Liliana: ¿Qué pasó? Ustedes solían ser uña y carne.

Vivian: Bueno, al principio todo estaba bien. Pero **poco a poco** las cosas empezaron a empeorar. Ramón estaba siempre **de un humor de perros**. Pero **la gota que derramó el vaso** fue que él nunca pagaba por nada y él sabe que **ando escasa de fondos**. Estas vacaciones me **costaron un ojo de la cara** pero él nunca quería **ir a medias**. Por fin, yo **puse las cartas sobre la mesa** y le dije que estaba arruinándome mis vacaciones, pero ¡**no le importó un bledo**!

Liliana: ¡Nunca me di cuenta de lo tacaño que es!

Vivian: Has **dado en el clavo**. Tengo que **hacer frente** al hecho de que no siempre puedes irte de vacaciones con tu mejor amigo.

Liliana: Bueno, **a despecho** de lo que pasó, espero que **hagan las paces** pronto.

Vivian: **Lo dicho, dicho**. No quiero verle más. Tenía tantas ganas de **hacer puente**. Ahora ¡**No puedo más**!

Lesson Eight

Liliana: So, **bring me up-to-date**. How was your vacation with Ramón? I'll bet you had a great time!

Vivian: **Far from it**. It was horrible **from beginning to end**. I was **on the verge** of **packing my bags** and coming home the next day...or telling him to **take a flying leap**. I **don't want anything to do with him** again!

Liliana: What happened? You too used to be close friends.

Vivian: Well, at first everything was fine. But **little by little**, things got worse. Ramón was constantly **in a lousy mood**. But the **last straw** was that he never paid for anything and he knows I'm **short of money**. This vacation ended up **costing an arm and a leg** because he wouldn't **split the cost** on anything. I finally **put my cards on the table** and told him that he was ruining my vacation but **he didn't give a darn**!

Liliana: I never realized how cheap he was!

Vivian: You **hit the nail on the head**. I have to **face up to** the fact that you can't always take a vacation with your best friend.

Liliana: Well, **in spite of** what happened, I hope you'll **make up** soon.

Vivian: **What I've said stands**. I don't want to see him again. I was looking so forward to **taking a long weekend** and relaxing. Now, **I'm exhausted**!

I sent him to go take a bath!

Liliana: So, **bring me to the day**. How was your vacation with Ramón? I'll bet you had a great time!

Vivian: **Not even much less**. It was horrible **from end to tail**. I was **at point of making my luggage** and coming home the next day...or sending him to **go take a bath**. I **don't want to have anything to see with him** again!

Liliana: What happened? You too used to be close friends.

Vivian: Well, at first everything was fine. But **little to little**, things got worse. Ramón was constantly **in a mood of dogs**. But the **drop that makes the glass spill over** was that he never paid for anything and he knows I'm **lacking funds**. This vacation ended up **costing an eye from the face** because he wouldn't **go halves** on anything. I finally **put the cards on the table** and told him that he was ruining my vacation but **it didn't matter to him one goosefoot plant**!

Liliana: I never realized how cheap he was!

Vivian: You **hit on the nail**. I have to **make the front to** the fact that you can't always take a vacation with your best friend.

Liliana: Well, **in spite of** what happened, I hope you'll **make peace** soon.

Vivian: **I said it, said**. I don't want to see him again. I was looking so forward to **making a bridge** and relaxing. Now, **I'm unable to do anything more**!

Vocabulary

a despecho de *exp.* in spite of • (lit.): to spite of.

> *example:* Bueno **a despecho de** lo que pasó espero que sigamos siendo amigos.
>
> *translation:* Well, **in spite of** what happened I hope we are still friends.

a punto de *exp.* on the point of; on the verge of, about to • (lit.): at point of.

> *example:* Estuve **a punto de** decirle lo que pienso de él.
>
> *translation:* I was **on the verge of** telling him what I think about him.
>
> **ALSO -1:** **a tal punto** *exp.* to such point • (lit.): to such a point.
>
> **ALSO -2:** **al punto** *exp.* at once • (lit.): to the point.
>
> **ALSO -3:** **en punto** *exp.* on time, on the dot • (lit.): in point.
>
> **ALSO -4:** **estar en su punto** *exp.* to be just right • (lit.): to be in its point.
>
> **ALSO -5:** **punto por punto** *exp.* in detail • (lit.): point by point.

costar un ojo de la cara *exp.* to cost an arm and a leg • (lit.): to cost an eye from the face.

> *example:* Ese abrigo **me costó un ojo de la cara**.
>
> *translation:* That coat **cost me an arm and a leg**.
>
> **SYNONYM -1:** **costar un huevo** *exp.* (Venezuela, Colombia, Bolivia, Ecuador, Peru, Spain) • (lit.): to cost an egg.
>
> > **NOTE:** This common expression is somewhat rude since the masculine noun *huevo* is commonly used to mean "testicle" in many Spanish-speaking countries.

SYNONYM -2: **costar un huevo y medio** *exp.* • (lit.): to cost an egg and a half.

> **NOTE:** This is a variation of the previous expression and is equally common.

dar en el clavo *exp.* to hit the nail on the head, to put one's finger on it • (lit.): to hit on the nail.

> *example:* ¡Tienes razón! ¡Has **dado en el clavo**!

> *translation:* You're right! You just **hit the nail on the head**!

SYNONYM: **dar el hito** *exp.* • (lit.): to hit on the stone.

> **NOTE -1:** **dar en** *exp.* to hit on • (lit.): to give on.

> **NOTE -2:** **dar con [algo]** *exp.* to find [something] • (lit.): to give with [something].

ALSO: **ser capaz de clavar un clavo con la cabeza** *exp.* to be pigheaded, stubborn • (lit.): to be capable of hammering a nail with the head.

de cabo a rabo *exp.* from beginning to end • (lit.): from end to tail.

> *example:* Me leí "El Quijote" **de cabo a rabo**.

> *translation:* I read "Don Quixote" **from beginning to end**.

SYNONYM -1: **de cabo a cabo** *exp.* • (lit.): from end to end.

SYNONYM -2: **de punta a punta** *exp.* • (lit.): from point to point.

ALSO -1: **al cabo** *exp.* at last • (lit.): at the end.

ALSO -2: **atar cabos** *exp.* to put two and two together • (lit.): to tie ends.

ALSO -3: **llevar a cabo** *exp.* to carry out • (lit.): to carry to end.

ALSO -4: **no dejar [un] cabo suelto** *exp.* not to leave any lose ends • (lit.): not to leave a loose end.

de un humor de perros (estar) *exp.* to be in a lousy mood • (lit.): to be in a mood of dogs.

> *example:* **¡Estoy de un humor de perros** porque alguien me robó mi bicicleta!

> *translation:* **I'm in a lousy mood** because someone stole my bicycle today!

> **SYNONYM:** **tener malas pulgas** *exp.* • (lit.): to have bad fleas • SEE: *p. 65.*

> **NOTE:** The expression *de perros* meaning "lousy" can be used to modify other nouns as well. A variation of *de perros* is *perro/a.* For example: *Pasé una noche perra;* I had a hell of a night.

> **ALSO -1:** **a otro perro con ese hueso** *exp.* don't give me that baloney, get out of here, come off it • (lit.): to another dog with that bone.

> **ALSO -2:** **perro viejo** *exp.* cunning and experienced individual, sly old dog • (lit.): old dog.

escaso/a de fondos (estar/andar) *exp.* to be short of money • (lit.): to lack funds.

> *example:* No puedo ir contigo al cine porque **estoy escaso de fondos**.

> *translation:* I can't go with you to the movies because I'm **short of money**.

> **SYNONYM -1:** **no tener ni un duro** *exp. (Spain)* • (lit.): no to have even a *duro*.

> > **NOTE:** **duro** *m.* a coin equal to five pesetas which is the national currency of Spain.

> **SYNONYM -2:** **no tener plata** *exp. (South America)* • (lit.): not to have any silver.

> **ANTONYM -1:** **estar podrido/a en dinero** *exp.* to be fithy-rich • (lit.): to be rotten in money.

> **ANTONYM -2:** **tener más lana que un borrego** *exp.* to have more wool than a lamb.

hacer el equipaje *exp.* to pack one's bags • (lit.): to make one's luggage.

> *example:* Estoy **haciendo el equipaje** para ir a España.

> *translation:* I'm **packing my bags** to go to Spain.

> **SYNONYM -1:** **empacar los belices** *exp. (Mexico)* • (lit.): to pack the bags.

> **SYNONYM -2:** **hacer las maletas** *exp.* • (lit.): to make one's trunks.

hacer frente a *exp.* to face up • (lit.): to make the front to.

> *example:* Tenemos que **hacer frente** al hecho de que nuestra empresa está perdiendo dinero.
>
> *translation:* We have **to face up to** the fact that our company is losing money.
>
> **ALSO -1:** **dar frente a** *exp.* to face • (lit.): to give the front • *Mi oficina da frente al lago;* My office faces the lake.
>
> **ALSO -2:** **frente a** *exp.* • **1.** across from. **2.** in the face of • (lit.): front to.
>
> **ALSO -3:** **frente a frente** *exp.* face to face • (lit.): forehead to forehead.

hacer las paces *exp.* to make up after a quarrel • (lit.): to make peace.

> *example:* Josefina y Gerardo se pelearon pero luego **hicieron las paces**.
>
> *translation:* Joesphina and Geraldo had a big fight but they finally **made up**.
>
> **SYNONYM:** **echar pelillos a la mar** *exp. (Southern Spain)* to throw little hairs to the sea.
>
> **ANTONYM:** **romper con** *exp.* to have a falling out • (lit.): to break with.

hacer puente *exp.* to take a long weekend, to take a three-day weekend • (lit.): to make a bridge.

> *example:* La próxima semana voy a **hacer puente** y voy a ir a esquiar.
>
> *translation:* Next week I'm going to take **a long weekend** and go skiing.

ir a medias *exp.* to split the cost of something, to go Dutch • (lit.): to go halves.

> *example:* Cuando salimos a cenar siempre **vamos a medias**.
>
> *translation:* When we go out for dinner we always **go Dutch**.
>
> **SYNONYM -1:** **ir a la mitad** *exp.* • (lit.): to go to the half.
>
> **SYNONYM -2:** **ir mitad mitad** *exp.* • (lit.): to go half-half.

la gota que derrama el vaso (ser) *exp.* to be the last straw, the straw that broke the camel's back • (lit.): to be the drop that makes the glass spill over.

> *example:* Elle me mintió anoche. ¡Eso ya **fue la gota que derramó el vaso**!
>
> *translation:* She lied to me last night. That's **the last straw**!

SYNONYM -1: **es el colmo** *exp.* • (lit.): it is the height (or: that's the limit).

SYNONYM -2: **la última gota que hace rebosar la copa** *exp.* • (lit.): the last drop that makes the glass overflow.

SYNONYM -3: **¡No faltaba más! / ¡Lo que faltaba! / ¡Sólo faltaba eso!** *exp.* • (lit.): Nothing else was missing! / What was missing! / Only that was missing!

SYNONYM -4: **la gota que colmó el vaso (ser)** *exp.* • (lit.): to be the drop that makes the glass spill over.

lo dicho, dicho *exp.* what I said, goes • (lit.): I said it, said.

> *example:* ¡Ya no te quiero ver más! **Lo dicho, dicho.**
>
> *translation:* I don't want to see you again! **What I said, goes.**

mandar a alguien a bañar *exp.* to tell someone to go take a flying leap, to tell someone to go fly a kite • (lit.): to send someone to take a bath.

> *example (1):* **¡Vete a bañar**!
>
> *translation:* **Go fly a kite**!
>
> *example (2):* Cuando Adolfo me pidió dinero por tercera vez, ¡**lo mandé a bañar**!
>
> *translation:* When Adolfo asked me to lend him money for the third time, I told him **to go take a flying leap**!

SYNONYM -1: **¡Vete a echar pulgas a otra parte!** *exp.* • (lit.): Go throw fleas somewhere else.

SYNONYM -2: **¡Vete a freír chongos!** *exp. (Mexico)* • (lit.): Go fry buns!

SYNONYM -3: **¡Vete a freír esparragos!** *exp.* • (lit.): Go fry asparagus.

SYNONYM -4: ¡**Vete a freír mocos!** *exp. (Ecuador, Peru, Bolivia)* • (lit.): Go fry mucus!

SYNONYM -5: ¡**Vete a freír monos!** *exp. (Colombia & Spain)* • (lit.): Go fry monkeys!

SYNONYM -6: ¡**Vete a ver si ya puso la cochina/puerca!** *exp. (Latin America)* • (lit.): Go see if the sow has already laid an egg.

ni mucho menos *exp.* far from it • (lit.): not even much less.

  example: ¿Lo pasaste bien en la fiesta? **Ni mucho menos**.

  translation: Did you have a good time at the party? **Far from it**.

  SYNONYM: ¡**Qué va!** *exp. (Spain)*• (lit.): What goes!

no importar un bledo *exp.* not to give a darn about [something] • (lit.): it doesn't matter one goosefoot plant.

  example: Irene no me invitó a su fiesta. Pero a mí **no me importa un bledo**. A mí mo me gusta ella de todas maneras.

  translation: Irena didn't invite me to her party. But I **don't give a darn**. I don't like her anyway.

  SYNONYM: **no importar un huevo** *exp.* • (lit.): it doesn't matter one egg.

    NOTE: This expression is somewhat rude and should be used with caution since *huevo* (literally meaning "egg") means "testicle" in many Spanish-speaking countries.

no poder más *exp.* to be exhausted • (lit.): to be unable to do more.

  example: ¡**No puedo más**! Me voy a dormir.

  translation: **I'm exhausted**! I'm going to sleep.

  SYNONYM -1: **estar más muerto/a que vivo/a** *exp.* • (lit.): to be more dead than alive.

  SYNONYM -2: **estar molido/a** *adj.* to be ground up or pulverized.

  SYNONYM -3: **estar muerto/a** *adj.* to be dead (tired).

  SYNONYM -4: **tener los huesos molidos** *exp.* • (lit.): to have one's bones ground up (or more literally: to be tired to the bone) • SEE: *p. 125.*

no querer tener nada que ver con alguien *exp.* not want to have anything to do with someone • (lit.): not to want to have anything to see with someone.

> *example:* **No quiero tener nada que ver con** Rigoberto porque está loco.
>
> *translation:* **I don't want to have anything to do with** Rigoberto because he's crazy.
>
> **SYNONYM:** **no querer liarse con alguien** *exp.* • (lit.): not to want to get involved with someone.

poco a poco *exp.* little by little • (lit.): little to little.

> *example:* **Poco a poco** terminé todo el proyecto.
>
> *translation:* **Little by little** I finished the whole project.
>
> **ALSO -1:** **¡a poco!** *exp. (Mexico)* really! • (lit.): to little!
>
> **ALSO -2:** **dentro de poco** *exp.* in a little while • (lit.): inside of little • SEE: *p. 159.*
>
> **ALSO -3:** **por poco** *exp.* almost • (lit.): by little.
>
> **ALSO -4:** **y por si fuera poco** *exp.* and as if that weren't enough • (lit.): and if that weren't little.

poner al día *exp.* to bring up-to-date, to inform, to give the lowdown • (lit.): to bring to the day.

> *example:* Pedro, ¡te voy a **poner al día**! Han pasado muchas cosas desde que te fuiste de vacaciones.
>
> *translation:* Pedro, I'm going **to bring you up-to-date**! A lot of things happened while you were on vacation.
>
> **SYNONYM:** **poner al tanto** *exp.* • (lit.): to put one at the point (in a score).
>
> **ALSO -1:** **corriente** *f.* trend • *las últimas corrientes de la moda;* the latest fashion trends.
>
> **ALSO -2:** **llevarle/seguirle la corriente a uno** *exp.* to humor someone, to go right along with that which is being said • (lit.): to carry/to follow the current to someone.

poner las cartas sobre la mesa *exp.* to to put one's cards on the table • (lit.): to put the cards on the table.

> *example:*   Si vas a hablar conmigo, **pon las cartas sobre la mesa**.
>
> *translation:*   If you're going to talk to me, **put all your cards on the table**.
>
> **ALSO:**   **tomar cartas en el asunto** *exp.* to take care of business • (lit.): to take cards in the business.

Practice the Vocabulary

(Answers to Lesson Eight, p. 203)

A. Choose the correct synonym of the word(s) in boldface.

1. **hacer puente**:
   a. to build a bridge
   b. to take a long weekend

2. **dar en el clavo**:
   a. to hit the nail on the head
   b. to say the wrong thing

3. **no importar a alguien un bledo**:
   a. not to give a darn
   b. to care a lot

4. **costar un ojo de la cara**:
   a. to be very inexpensive
   b. to be very expensive

5. **ir escasa de fondos**:
   a. to have a lot of money
   b. to have little money

6. **un humor de perros**:
   a. to be in a lousy mood
   b. to be in a very good mood

7. **ir a medias**:
   a. to go Dutch
   b. to pay cash

8. **hacer el equipaje**:
   a. to pack
   b. to unpack

9. **mandar a alguien a bañar**:
   a. to tell someone to take a flying leap
   b. to tell someone to stay

10. **hacer frente**:
    a. to turn one's back on someone
    b. to face up to something

11. **poner a alguien al corriente**:
    a. to bring someone up-to-date
    b. to lie to someone

12. **hacer las paces**:
    a. to fight
    b. to make up

B. Complete the following phrases by choosing the appropriate word(s) from the list below. Make all necessary changes.

cuestan un ojo de la cara   no puedo más
da en el clavo   no quiero nada que ver
de cabo a rabo   poco a poco
hacer el equipaje   pon las cartas sobre la mesa
hacer las paces   ponme al corriente
ni mucho menos   un humor de perros

1. Después de dormir la siesta me levanto con
   _____.

2. Los relojes de Cartier _____.

3. Sé claro de una vez y _____.

4. _____ con él; es un antipático.

5. A Juan le gusta leer el periódico _____.

6. Lo más bonito después de una pelea es _____.

7. Mis vacaciones con Marisa no fueron buenas _____.

8. _____ las cosas fueron mejorando.

9. Cada vez que Pedro dice algo, _____.

10. Ya _____, llevo todo el día trabajando.

11. Me gusta _____ una semana antes de salir de viaje.

12. _____ de como fueron tus vacaciones en
    Cancún.

C. Underline the appropriate word(s) that best complete(s) the phrase.

1. Las vacaciones terminaron (**costando un ojo de la cara**, **costando la cara**, **costando dos ojos**).

2. Me gustaría oírte contar la historia (**sin cabos**, **de cabo a rabo**, **de rabo a cabo**).

3. (**Quiero más**, **sin poder más**, **no puedo más**), hace una calor insoportable.

4. Siempre se va solo al cine, yo (**no le bledo**, **no le importo un bledo**, **le importo bledos**).

5. Espero que solucionéis las cosas (**a despecho de**, **sin pecho de**, **despecho**) lo que os pasó.

6. A Pedro le apetece muchísimo (**equipar el equipaje**, **hacer el equipaje**, **hacer**) e irse de viaje.

7. Que Jorge nunca se quejara fue (**la última gota**, **el vaso derramado**, **la gota que derramó el vaso**).

8. Tengo que (**ponerte al corriente**, **ir contra corriente**, **es muy corriente**) de las últimas novedades.

9. A mis padres no le importa que vengas a casa y (**ni menos**, **ni mucho menos**, **más o menos**) que te quedes.

10. Vamos a pagar (**a medias**, **con una media**, **mediar**); así es más fácil.

11. ¡Estoy (**de perros**, **de un humor de gatos**, **de un humor de perros**)! Otra vez se me ha estropeado la moto.

12. El jueves es fiesta, así que en la oficina hemos decidido (**hacer un puente**, **hacer puente**, **construir un puente**) y no volver hasta el lunes.

D. Complete the dialogue using the list below.

a costar un ojo de la cara	hacer frente
de cabo a rabo	ir a medias
de un humor de perros	la gota que derramó el vaso
escasa de fondos	no puede más
está a punto de hacer	poco a poco
hacer el equipaje	ponme al corriente

Vivian: ¿Te has enterado de lo que ha ocurrido en Badajoz?

Liliana: No, _____. Cuéntame todo _____.

Vivian: Hace unos días hubo una tormenta terrible; trece muertos en total.

Pero _____ es el hecho de que la

catástrofe ocurrió en un barrio obrero, que no contaba con la

infraestructura adecuada. Como comprenderás la gente está

_____.

Liliana: ¿Por qué? ¿Hay responsables?

Vivian: Bueno, en realidad es posible que los haya, pues se trata de una

comunidad _____, y el ayuntamiento encima no ha

hecho nada al respecto. Creo que el alcalde va a tener que

_____ y largarse. El gobierno local y el central se

han comprometido a _____ en las reparaciones. En

estos momentos, el presidente _____ unas

declaraciones al respecto. Creo que les va _____

volver a la normalidad.

Liliana: ¡Qué horror! Además, esa zona es bastante seca y no están nada

preparados para estas situaciones. Espero que _____

todo se resuelva.

Vivian: Sí, alguien va a tener que _____ a la situación; la gente

_____.

E. DICTATION
Test Your Aural Comprehension

(This dictation can be found in the Appendix on page 212.)

If you are following along with your cassette, you will now hear a series of sentences from the opening dialogue. These sentences will be read by a native speaker at normal conversational speed (which may seem fast to you at first). In addition, the words will be pronounced as you would actually hear them in a conversation, often including some common reductions.

The first time the sentences are presented, simply listen in order to get accustomed to the speed and heavy use of reductions. The sentences will then be read again with a pause after each to give you time to write down what you heard. The third time the sentences are read, follow along with what you have written.

¡Ricardo me ha dejado plantada!

(trans.): Richard **stood me up**!
(lit.): Richard **left me planted**!

¡Ricardo me ha dejado plantada!

Verónica: ¿Cómo estás?

Lucia: **Así, así**. Creo que Ricardo **me ha dejado plantada**. Debería de haber estado aquí hace diez minutos. ¡Los hombres me **dan tanta rabia**! Creo que no le gusto.

Verónica: Eso **no tiene ni pies ni cabeza**. Estoy segura que va a llegar **dentro de poco**.

Lucia: ¡No te lo **tomes a broma**! Ya pasó una vez y **por ningún motivo** voy a dejar que pase otra vez. Yo **no tengo ni un pelo de tonta**. Simplemente le tengo que **hacer frente al hecho** de que él no va a venir. ¡Qué lástima! **Hasta la fecha** nunca había conocido a nadie como él.

Verónica: ¡Un momento! Tú misma me dijiste que **por lo general** él nunca llega **de antemano**. ¿Por qué no le puedes **tomar la palabra**? Lo más seguro es que esté manejando **a toda prisa a fin de** llegar aquí lo antes posible. Además, a lo mejor se le hizo tarde, hay mucho tráfico, tuvo una emergencia, o **algo por el estilo**.

Lucia: Bueno, eso es **harina de otro costal**. No se me había ocurrido eso.

Verónica: **De un modo u otro**, seguro que se presentará. ¡Mira! ¡Allí está! ¡**Más vale tarde que nunca**!

Lucia: ¡Yo sabía que él iba a venir!

Lesson Nine

Verónica: How are you?

Lucia: **So-so**. I think Ricardo **stood me up**. He was supposed to be here ten minutes ago. Men **make me so mad**! I don't think he likes me.

Verónica: **That doesn't make any sense**. I'm sure he's going to arrive **soon**.

Lucia: **Don't take this lightly**! It happened once before and **under no circumstance** will I let it happen again. I'm not **anyone's fool**. I just have **to face up to the fact that** he's not coming. What a shame! **So far**, I've never met anyone like him before.

Verónica: Now wait! You told me yourself that **as a general rule**, he never arrives **ahead of time**. Why can't you **take him at his word**? He's probably driving **at full speed in order to** get here as soon as he can. Besides, he may have gotten a late start, hit traffic, had an emergency, or **something like that**.

Lucia: Well, **that's a horse of a different color**. I hadn't thought of that.

Verónica: **In one way or another**, he'll be here. Look! There he is! **Better late than never**!

Lucia: I always knew he'd come!

Richard left me planted!

Verónica: How are you?

Lucia: **So-so**. I think Ricardo **left me planted**. He was supposed to be here ten minutes ago. Men **make me so mad**! I don't think he likes me.

Verónica: **That doesn't have feet or head**. I'm sure he's going to arrive **soon**.

Lucia: **Don't take this like a joke**! It happened once before and **by no reason** will I let it happen again. I don't **have even one hair of stupid**. I just have **to face up to the fact that** he's not coming. What a shame! **Until that date** I've never met anyone like him before.

Verónica: Now wait! You told me yourself that **generally**, he never arrives **of beforehand**. Why can't you **take the word to him**? He's probably driving **at all speed to end of** get here as soon as he can. Besides, he may have gotten a late start, hit traffic, had an emergency, or **something of the same style**.

Lucia: Well, **that's flour of a different sack**. I hadn't thought of that.

Verónica: **In one way or another**, he'll be here. Hey, there he is! **It's worth more late than never**!

Lucia: I always knew he'd come!

Vocabulary

a fin de *exp.* in order to • (lit.): to end of.

    example: Voy a comer menos **a fin de** perder peso.

    translation: I'm going to eat less **in order to** lose weight.

    SYNONYM: **con el fin de** *exp.* • (lit.): with the end of.

    ALSO -1: **a fin de cuentas** *exp.* after all • (lit.): to end of accounts.

    ALSO -2: **al fin y al cabo** *exp.* after all • (lit.): at the end and at the end.

    ALSO -3: **en fin** *exp.* in short • (lit.): in end.

    ALSO -4: **por fin** *exp.* at last • (lit.): by end.

    ALSO -5: **un sin fin de** *exp.* no end of • (lit.): a without end of.

así, así *exp.* so, so • (lit.): such, such.

    example: ¿Te gustan las películas de miedo? **Así, así**.

    translation: Do you like horror movies? **So, so**.

a toda prisa *exp.* at full speed, as quickly as possible • (lit.): at all speed.

    example: Voy a la escuela **a toda prisa** porque me levanté tarde.

    translation: I'm going to school **at full speed** because I woke up late.

    SYNONYM -1: **a toda vela** *exp.* • (lit.): at all sail.

    SYNONYM -2: **a todo meter** *exp.* (*Southern Spain*) • (lit.): at all introduce.

SYNONYM -3:	**en un avemaría** *exp.* • (lit.): in one Hail Mary.
SYNONYM -4:	**en un chiflido** *exp.* • (lit.): in one whistle.
SYNONYM -5:	**en un credo** *exp.* • (lit.): in one creed.
SYNONYM -6:	**en un decir Jesús** *exp.* • (lit.): in one saying of Jesus.
SYNONYM -7:	**en un dos por tres** *exp.* • (lit.): in a two by three.
SYNONYM -8:	**en un improviso** *exp. (Colombia, Venezuela, Mexico)* • (lit.): in one sudden action.
SYNONYM -9:	**en un salto** *exp.* • (lit.): in one leap.
SYNONYM -10:	**en un soplo** *exp.* • (lit.): in a gust or blow.

algo por el estilo *exp.* something like that, similar. • (lit.): something of the same style.

> *example:* Esa casa es **algo por el estilo** a la mía.
>
> *translation:* That house **is similar** to mine.
>
> **SYNONYM:** **cosas por el estilo** *exp.* • (lit.): things of the same style.
>
> **ALSO -1:** **algo es algo** *exp.* it's better than nothing • (lit.): something is something.
>
> **ALSO -3:** **por algo** *exp.* no wonder • (lit.): by something • *Antonio trabajo mucho. ¡Por algo tiene tanto dinero!;* Antonio works a lot. No wonder he has so much money!

dar [tanta] rabia *exp.* to make one [so] mad • (lit.): to give rage.

> *example:* **Me da tanta rabia** cuando la gente llega tarde a una cita.
>
> *translation:* **It gets me so ticked off** when people arrive late to an appointment.
>
> **ALSO:** **tener rabia a** *exp.* to have a grudge against • (lit.): to have rage to.

de antemano *exp.* ahead of time • (lit.): of beforehand.

> *example:* Yo siempre llego a mi trabajo **de antemano**.
>
> *translation:* I always arrive at my work **ahead of time**.

dejar plantado/a a alguien *exp.* to stand someone up, to leave in the lurch • (lit.): to leave someone planted.

>   *example:*   ¡No lo puedo creer! ¡Verónica **me dejó plantado**!

>   *translation:*   I can't believe it! Veronica **stood me up**!

dentro de poco *exp.* any moment, soon • (lit.): in a little bit.

>   *example:*   Carlos llegará **dentro de poco**.

>   *translation:*   Carlos will arrive **any moment**.

de un modo u otro *exp.* one way or another • (lit.): of a way or another

>   *example:*   **De un modo u otro** iré a visitarte este verano.

>   *translation:*   **One way or another** I'll visit you next summer.

hacer frente al hecho *exp.* to face up to the fact that • (lit.): to face up to the fact.

>   *example:*   Tengo que **hacerle frente al hecho** de que tengo que trabajar tarde esta noche.

>   *translation:*   I have **to face up to the fact that** I have to work late tonight.

>   **SYNONYM:**   **dar la cara a** *exp.* • (lit.): to give the face to.

harina de otro costal (ser) *exp.* to be another story, to be a horse of a different color • (lit.): to be flour of a different sack.

>   *example:*   ¡Eso es **harina de otro costal**!

>   *translation:*   That's **a different story**!

>   **SYNONYM -1:**   **no tener que ver con nada** *exp.* • (lit.): not to have anything to do with anything.

>   **SYNONYM -2:**   **no venir al cuento** *exp.* • (lit.): not to come to the story.

>   **SYNONYM -3:**   **ser otro cantar** *exp.* • (lit.): to be another song.

hasta la fecha *exp.* to date, up till now • (lit.): until that date.

> *example:* **Hasta la fecha** nunca había comido un pescado tan delicioso.
>
> *translation:* **Up till now**, I have never had such delicious fish.
>
> **SYNONYM -1:** **hasta el día de hoy** *exp.* • (lit.): until today.
>
> **SYNONYM -2:** **hasta hoy** *exp.* • (lit.): until today.
>
> **SYNONYM -3:** **hasta la actualidad** *exp.* • (lit.): until today.

más vale tarde que nunca *exp.* better late than never • (lit.): it is worth more late than never.

> *example:* Menos mal que llegaste. **Más vale tarde que nunca**.
>
> *translation:* Good thing you showed up. **Better late than never**.

no tener ni pies ni cabeza *exp.* not to make any sense • (lit.): not to have feet or head.

> *example:* Lo que estás diciendo **no tiene ni pies ni cabeza**.
>
> *translation:* What you're saying **doesn't make any sense**.

no tener ni un pelo de tonto/a *exp.* to be nobody's fool • (lit.): not to have even one hair of stupid.

> *example:* Pedro **no tiene ni un pelo de tonto**.
>
> *translation:* Pedro is **nobody's fool**.
>
> **SYNONYM:** **ser muy vivo/a** *exp.* *(Mexico)* • (lit.): to be very alive.

por lo general *exp.* as a general rule, usually • (lit.): generally.

> *example:* **Por lo general** no me gusta comer mucha carne roja.
>
> *translation:* **As a general rule**, I don't like to eat too much red meat.
>
> **SYNONYM -1:** **por lo común** *exp.* • (lit.): by the common.
>
> **SYNONYM -2:** **por lo regular** *exp.* • (lit.): by the regular.

por ningún motivo *exp.* under no circumstances • (lit.): by no reason.

> *example:* **Por ningún motivo** me hables en ese tono de voz.
>
> *translation:* **Under no circumstances** are you to talk to me using that tone of voice.
>
> **SYNONYM:** **bajo ningún motivo** *exp.* • (lit.): under no reason.
>
> **ALSO -1:** **con motivo de** *exp.* on the occasion of [an event] • (lit.): with reason of.
>
> **ALSO -2:** **por motivo de** *exp.* on account of • (lit.): by reason of.

tomar a broma *exp.* to take lightly • (lit.): to take like a joke.

> *example:* ¡**No te lo tomes a broma**! Estoy hablado en serio.
>
> *translation:* **Don't take it lightly**! I'm serious.
>
> **ANTONYM:** **tomar en serio** *exp.* to take it seriously • (lit.): to take it seriously.
>
> **ALSO -1:** **bromas aparte** *exp.* all joking aside • (lit.): jokes to the side.
>
> **ALSO -2:** **hacer una broma** *exp.* to play a joke • (lit.): to make a joke.
>
> **ALSO -3:** **no estar para bromas** *exp.* to be in no mood for jokes • (lit.): not to be for jokes.

tomarle la palabra a alguien *exp.* to take someone at his/her word • (lit.): to take the word to someone.

> *example:* Está bien. Voy a **tomarte la palabra**.
>
> *translation:* O.K. I'm going **to take you at your word**.
>
> **ALSO -1:** **en otras palabras** *exp.* in other words • (lit.): [same].
>
> **ALSO -2:** **tener la palabra** *exp.* to have the floor • (lit.): to have the word.

Practice the Vocabulary

(Answers to Lesson Nine, p. 204)

A. Underline the definition of the word(s) in boldface.

1. **algo por el estilo**:
   a. something like that
   b. nothing like that

2. **por lo general**:
   a. occasionally
   b. as a general rule

3. **a toda prisa**:
   a. at full speed
   b. very slowly

4. **me ha dejado plantado/a**:
   a. I planted a tree
   b. he/she stood me up

5. **más vale tarde que nunca**:
   a. it's already too late
   b. better late than never

6. **por ningún motivo**:
   a. under no circumstances
   b. for sure

7. **tomar(le) la palabra**:
   a. to take someone at his/her word
   b. not to pay attention

8. **dentro de poco**:
   a. any moment
   b. yesterday

9. **hacer frente al hecho**:
   a. to face the fact
   b. to avoid the fact

10. **de antemano**:
    a. ahead of time
    b. much later

11. **tomar a broma**:
    a. to take something seriously
    b. to take something lightly

12. **dar tanta rabia**:
    a. to make someone mad
    b. to make someone happy

B. Complete the following phrases by choosing the appropriate word(s) from the list below. Make all necessary changes.

a fin de	**me ha dejado plantado**
a toda prisa	**no tiene ni pies ni cabeza**
así, así	**no tiene ni un pelo de tonta**
da tanta rabia	**por lo general**
hacer frente al hecho de	**por ningún motivo**
hasta la fecha	**ya es harina de otro costal**

1. Lo que estás diciendo _____.

2. María _____; sabe muy bien lo que hace.

3. _____ nunca había conocido a nadie tan simpático.

4. La policía interrogó a todos los testigos _____ descubrir la verdad.

5. Juan dijo que la fiesta del viernes estuvo _____.

6. Tienes que _____ que Marisa no quiere estar contigo.

7. Si no vamos _____, no llegaremos a tiempo de ver la película empezar.

8. Ricardo no llega. Yo creo que _____.

9. _____ Beatriz es muy simpática, pero hoy estaba de mal humor.

10. No me importa dejarte mi moto, pero la de mi padre _____.

11. Me _____ ver una película empezada, que prefiero no verla.

12. _____ voy a perdonarle, ya es la segunda vez que llega tarde.

C. Match the English phrase in the left column with the Spanish translation from the right. Mark the appropriate letter in the box.

☐ 1. I am going to Spain soon.

☐ 2. To tell you the truth, I am feeling so-so.

☐ 3. I would like to buy something like that.

☐ 4. One way or another you'll have to pay us a visit.

☐ 5. I'm serious. Don't take this lightly.

☐ 6. Jorge and Carmen saved money for five years in order to buy a house.

☐ 7. As of today, I haven't gotten a single letter from Javier.

☐ 8. Antonio is nobody's fool.

☐ 9. I warned him ahead of time.

☐ 10. His speech didn't make any sense.

☐ 11. Manuel stood me up at the movie theater.

☐ 12. As soon as he heard the news, he went home at full speed.

A. Me gustaría comprar **algo por el estilo**.

B. Estoy hablando en serio. No te lo **tomes a broma**.

C. **Hasta la fecha** no he recibido ninguna carta de Javier.

D. Manuel **me dejó plantado** en la puerta del cine.

E. Se lo advertí **de antemano**.

F. En cuanto se enteró de la noticia, salió **a toda prisa** hacia su casa.

G. **De un modo u otro**, tienes que visitarnos.

H. **Dentro de poco** me voy a España.

I. Su discurso **no tuvo ni pies ni cabeza**.

J. Antonio **no tiene ni un pelo de tonto**.

K. Para serte sincero, me encuentro **así, así**.

L. Jorge y Carmen estuvieron ahorrando cinco años **a fin de** comprar una casa.

D. FIND-A-WORD PUZZLE
Using the list below, circle the words in the grid on page 167 that are missing from the Spanish idiom. Words may be spelled up, down, or across.

antemano	fin	plantado
cabeza	frente	prisa
costal	nunca	rabia
estilo	palabra	tonto

1. *example:* Voy a comer menos **a _____ de** perder peso.

   translation: I'm going to eat less **in order to** lose weight.

2. *example:* Voy a la escuela **a toda _____** porque me levanté tarde.

   translation: I'm going to school **at full speed** because I woke up late.

3. *example:* Esa casa es **algo por el _____** a la mía.

   translation: That house **is similar** to mine.

4. *example:* **Me da tanta _____** cuando la gente llega tarde a una cita.

   translation: **It gets me so ticked off** when people arrive late to an appoiment.

5. *example:* Yo siempre llego a mi trabajo **de _____**.

   translation: I always arrive at my work **ahead of time**.

6. *example:* ¡No lo puedo creer! ¡Verónica **me dejó _____**!

   translation: I can't believe it! Veronica **stood me up**!

7.   *example:*   Tengo que **hacerle** _____ **al hecho** de que tengo que trabajar esta noche.

      translation: I have **to face up to the fact that** I have to work tonight.

8.   *example:*   ¡Eso es **harina de otro** _____!

      translation: That's **a different story**!

9.   *example:*   Menos mal que llegaste. **Más vale tarde que _____.**

      translation: Good thing you showed up. **Better late than never**.

10.   *example:*   Lo que estás diciendo **no tiene ni pies ni** _____.

      translation: What you're saying **doesn't make any sense**.

11.   *example:*   Pedro **no tiene ni un pelo de** _____.

      translation: Pedro is **nobody's fool**.

12.   *example:*   Está bien. Voy a **tomarte la** _____.

      translation: O.K. I'm going **to take you at your word**.

FIND-A-WORD CUBE

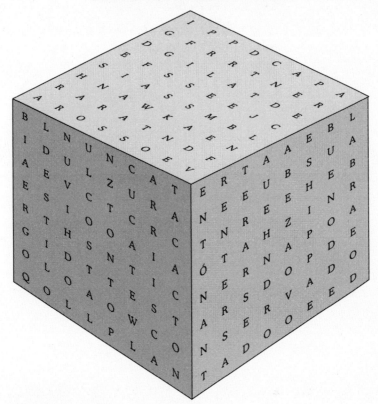

E. DICTATION
Test Your Aural Comprehension

(This dictation can be found in the Appendix on page 213.)

If you are following along with your cassette, you will now hear a series of sentences from the opening dialogue. These sentences will be read by a native speaker at normal conversational speed (which may seem fast to you at first). In addition, the words will be pronounced as you would actually hear them in a conversation, often including some common reductions.

The first time the sentences are presented, simply listen in order to get accustomed to the speed and heavy use of reductions. The sentences will then be read again with a pause after each to give you time to write down what you heard. The third time the sentences are read, follow along with what you have written.

LECCIÓN DIEZ

¡Se metió en un buen berenjenal!

(trans.): **He got himself into a real jam!**
(lit.): **He got himself into a good eggplant!**

¡Se metió en un buen berenjenal!

Laura:	Estoy **en brasas**. ¿Qué pasó?
Miguel:	Ernesto decidió **probar fortuna** en la lotería...y ¡ganó! ¡**Hizo su agosto**! Le vino **como llovido del cielo**. Teniendo en cuenta los millones de personas que jugaron esta vez, la verdad es que ganó **contra viento y marea**.
Laura:	¡Qué bien! **Se metió en un buen berenjenal** cuando perdió su trabajo el año pasado. Casi no podía **pagar la casa**. Ahora va a poder **ponerse a flote** otra vez. Debe de estar **afuera de sí**.
Miguel:	**No cabe de contento**. Ya sabes que se **jugó el todo por el todo** y que usó todos sus ahorros para comprar miles de boletos. **Por fortuna**, le fue bien. **Solía vivir al día** pero eso se terminó. Ahora podrá viajar **a lo largo y a lo ancho** del mundo. La verdad es que ha **nacido de pie**.
Laura:	Me preguntaba por qué **estaba de buenas** cuando le vi esta mañana. Bueno, ya sabes que seguro que no se le **sube a la cabeza**. Eso **va sin decir**.
Miguel:	Lo más seguro es que se gaste su dinero en los demás.
Laura:	Yo no estaría tan seguro de eso. ¡Me acaba de decir que se va a comprar un automóvil con **dinero contante y sonante**!
Miguel:	Bueno, una cosa es segura. ¡**Poderoso caballero es Don Dinero**!

Lesson Ten

Laura: I'm **on pins and needles**. What happened?

Miguel: Ernesto decided to **try his luck** at the lottery... and won! He **made a killing**! It came **like manna from heaven**. With the millions of people who were playing this time, he really won **against all odds**.

Laura: That's great! He **got himself into a real jam** when he lost his job last year. He almost didn't have enough money to **pay the rent**. Now he'll be able to **get on his feet** again. He must be **beside himself** with excitement!

Miguel: **He couldn't fit because he's so happy**. You know, he **risked every- thing** and used his entire savings to buy thousands of tickets! **Fortunately**, it paid off. He used to **live day to day**, but not any more. Now he'll be able to travel **throughout** the world. He sure was **born lucky**.

Laura: I wondered why he was in such a **good mood** when I saw him this morning. Well, you know this certainly won't **go to his head**. **That goes without saying**.

Miguel: He'll probably end up spending his money on everyone else.

Laura: I wouldn't be so sure. He just told me he's planning on buying a car with **cold hard cash**!

Miguel: Well, one thing is for sure... **money makes the world go 'round**!

He got himself into a good eggplant!

Laura: I'm **on live coal**. What happened?

Miguel: Ernesto decided to **to try fortune** at the lottery... and won! He **made his August**! It came **like rained from the sky**. With the millions of people who were playing this time, he really won **against wind and tide**.

Laura: That's great! He **got himself into a good eggplant** when he lost his job last year. He almost didn't have enough money to **pay the house**. Now he'll be able to **get himself afloat** again. He must be **out of himself** with excitement!

Miguel: **He couldn't be happier**. You know, he **played everything for everything** and used his entire savings to buy thousands of tickets! **By fortune**, it paid off. He used to **live to the day**, but not any more. Now he'll be able to travel **lengthwise and sideways** in the world. He sure was **born standing**.

Laura: I wondered why he was in such **good ones** when I saw him this morning. Well, you know this certainly won't **go up to his head**. **That goes without saying**.

Miguel: He'll probably end up spending his money on everyone else.

Laura: I wouldn't be so sure. He just told me he's planning on buying a car with **cash money and sounding**!

Miguel: Well, one thing is for sure... **Mr. Money is a powerful gentleman**!

Vocabulary

a lo largo y a lo ancho *exp.* throughout • (lit.): lengthwise and sideways.

> *example:* Manuel siempre ha tenido mucha suerte **a lo largo y a lo ancho** de su vida.

> *translation:* Manuel's always been very lucky **throughout** his life.

> **ALSO -1:** **ponerse muy ancho** *exp.* to become conceited or vain • (lit.): to become very wide.

> **ALSO -2:** **quedarse tan ancho** *exp.* not to worry, keep calm (about what has been said or done) • (lit.): to stay so wide.

afuera de sí (estar) *exp.* beside oneself • (lit.): out of oneself.

> *example:* Alberto parece **estar afuera de sí**. Que pasó?

> *translation:* Alberto seems **to be beside himself**. What happened?

> **SYNONYM:** **fuera de sí** *exp.* • (lit.): out of oneself.

no caber de contento *exp.* to be very happy, to be excited [about something] • (lit.): not to fit because one is so happy.

> *example:* Alfredo **no cabe de contento** porque tiene una novia nueva.

> *translation:* Alfredo **couldn't be happier** because he has a new girlfriend.

como llovido del cielo *exp.* like manna from heaven, heaven sent • (lit.): like rained from the sky.

> *example:*   Ese dinero me vino **como llovido del cielo**.
>
> *translation:*   That money came **like manna from heaven**.

contra viento y marea *exp.* against all odds • (lit.): against wind and tide.

> *example:*   La tortuga ganó la carrera **contra viento y marea**.
>
> *translation:*   The tortoise won the race **against all odds**.

dinero contante y sonante *exp.* cold hard cash • (lit.): cash money and sounding.

> *example:*   Alfonso pagó su casa con **dinero contante y sonante**.
>
> *translation:*   Alfonso paid for his house with **cold hard cash**.
>
> **SYNONYM -1:**   **dinero al contado** *exp.* • (lit.): counting money.
>
> **SYNONYM -2:**   **dinero en efectivo** *exp.* • (lit.): effective money.

en brasas (estar) *exp.* to be on pins and needles, to be on tenterhooks, be uneasy. • (lit.): to be in live coal.

> *example:*   Susan está esperando ver si le dieron su ascenso. ¡**Está en brasas**!
>
> *translation:*   Susan is waiting to see if she got a promotion. She's **is on pins and needles**!
>
> **SYNONYM:**   **estar como en brasas** *exp.* • (lit.): to be like in live coal.
>
> **ALSO:**   **estar hecho/a unas brasas** *exp.* to be red in the face, to be flushed • (lit.): to be made some live coal.
>
> **ALSO:**   **pasar como sobre brasas** *exp.* to touch very lightly on • (lit.): to pass like over live coal.

estar de buenas *exp.* to be in a good mood • (lit.): to be in good.

　　example: Lynda es una mujer muy feliz. Siempre **está de buenas**.

　　translation: Lynda is a very happy woman. She is always **in a good mood**.

ANTONYM -1:	**estar de malas** *exp.* to be in a bad mood • (lit.): to be in bad.
ANTONYM -2:	**estar de un humor de perros** *exp.* • (lit.): to be in the mood of dogs • SEE: **de un humor de perros (estar)**, *p. 140.*
ANTONYM -3:	**tener malas pulgas** *exp.* • (lit.): to have bad fleas.

hacer su agosto *exp.* to make a killing • (lit.): to make one's August.

　　example: Alfredo y Eva **hicieron su agosto** en el casino.

　　translation: Alfredo y Eva **made a killing** at the casino.

ir sin decir *exp.* to go without saying • (lit.): to go without saying.

　　example: Eso **va sin decir**.

　　translation: That **goes without saying**.

jugar el todo por el todo *exp.* to risk everything, to go for it • (lit.): to play (risk) everything for everything.

　　example: Cuando invertí en la bolsa, me **jugé el todo por el todo**.

　　translation: When I invested in the stock market, I **risked everything**.

meterse en un [buen] berenjenal *exp.* to get oneself into a [real] jam, to get oneself into a fine mess • (lit.): to get into a good eggplant patch.

　　example: No mientas sobre lo que pasó o te vas a **meter en un buen berenjenal**.

　　translation: Everytime I go to that bar **I get myself into a mess**.

| SYNONYM: | **meterse en un buen lío** *exp.* • (lit.): to put oneself in a good bundle. |

nacer de pie *exp.* to be born lucky • (lit.): to be born (on foot) standing.

> *example:* Yo he **nacido de pie**.
>
> *translation:* I was **born lucky**.
>
> **SYNONYM -1:** **nacer con estrella** *exp.* • (lit.): to be born with star.
> **SYNONYM -2:** **nacer parado/a** *exp.* • (lit.): to be born standing.
> **ANTONYM -1:** **nacer al revés** *exp.* to be born unlucky • (lit.): to be born backwards.
> **ANTONYM -2:** **nacer estrellado/a** *exp.* to be born unlucky • (lit.): to be born crashed.

pagar la casa *exp.* to pay rent • (lit.): to pay the house.

> *example:* No tengo dinero porque ayer **pagué la casa**.
>
> *translation:* I don't have any money because yesterday I **paid my rent**.

poderoso caballero es Don Dinero *exp.* money makes the world go 'round, money talks • (lit.): Mr. money is a powerful gentleman.

> *example:* Me dieron la mejor mesa del restaurante. **Poderoso caballero es Don Dinero**.
>
> *translation:* They gave me the best table in the restaurant. **Money makes the world go 'round**.
>
> **ALSO:** **nadar en dinero** *exp.* to be rolling in money • (lit.): to swim in money.

ponerse a flote *exp.* to get back up on one's own two feet again • (lit.): to put oneself afloat.

> *example:* Después de comenzar su nuevo trabajo, Alberto **se puso a flote** otra vez.
>
> *translation:* After starting his new job, Alberto is **back on his feet**.
>
> **SYNONYM:** **levantar la cabeza** *exp.* • (lit.): to lift the head.
>
> **NOTE:** This could be best compared to the American expression, "to hold up one's head" or "to pull oneself back up."

por fortuna *exp.* fortunately • (lit.): by fortune.

> *example:*   Hoy hubo una gran explosión en la fábrica pero **por fortuna** no hubo heridos.

> *translation:*   There was a big explosion at the factory today but **fortunately** no one was hurt.

probar fortuna *exp.* to try one's luck • (lit.): to try fortune.

> *example:*   Cuando voy a Las Vegas me gusta **probar fortuna** en el casino.

> *translation:*   When I go to Las Vegas I enjoy **trying my luck** in the casino.

> **ALSO:**   **tener buena fortuna** *exp.* to have good luck • (lit.): to have good fortune.

subir a la cabeza *exp.* • to go to one's head (said of conceit or alcohol) • (lit.): to go up to one's head.

> *example:*   Parece que a Arturo se le **subió a la cabeza** el hecho de que ahora es supervisor.

> *translation:*   It seems that the fact that Arturo is now a supervisor **went to his head**.

> **ALSO -1:**   **levantar la cabeza** *exp.* to get on one's feet • (lit.): to raise one's head.

> **ALSO -2:**   **perder la cabeza** *exp.* to lose one's head • (lit.): to lose one's head.

vivir al día *exp.* to live day to day, to live from hand to mouth • (lit.): to live to the day.

> *example:*   Mucha gente en este país **vive al día**.

> *translation:*   Many people in this country **live day to day**.

> **ALSO -1:**   **de día en día** *exp.* by the day • (lit.): from day to day.

> **ALSO -2:**   **del día** *exp.* today's • (lit.): from the day.

> **ALSO -3:**   **estar al día** *exp.* to be up-to-date • (lit.): to be to the day.

> **ALSO -4:**   **poner al día** *exp.* to bring up-to-date • (lit.): to put to the day.

> **ALSO -5:**   **todo el santo día** *exp.* all day long • (lit.): the whole holy day.

Practice the Vocabulary

(Answers to Lesson Ten, p. 206)

A. Fill in the blanks with the correct word(s) that best complete(s) the phrase.

a lo largo y ancho
como llovida del cielo
contra viento y marea
dinero contante y sonante
está de buenas
hizo su agosto
jugó el todo por el todo

metimos en un buen
  berenjenal
nacido de pie
por fortuna
probé fortuna
sube a la cabeza

1. Cuando fui al casino _____ en la ruleta y gané bastante dinero.

2. La cerveza se me _____.

3. Carlos defiende sus intereses _____.

4. La herencia me vino _____.

5. El día de la tormenta, el hombre que vendía paraguas _____.

6. He manejado _____ de este mundo.

7. Al final Alfonso se _____ y decidió decir la verdad.

8. Nos _____ cuando le dijimos al policía que era muy feo.

9. Antonio parece haber _____, tiene una suerte bárbara.

10. Lo pagó todo con _____.

11. Venga, pídele permiso para ir al cine. Hoy se le ve que _____.

12. _____, no pasó nada de lo que nos pudiéramos arrepentir.

B. Underline the definition of the words in boldface.

1. **ponerse a flote**:
   a. to get on one's feet
   b. to be unstable

2. **vivir al día**:
   a. to seize the day
   b. to live day to day

3. **en brasas (estar)**:
   a. to be calm
   b. to be on pins and needles

4. **pagar la casa**:
   a. to pay the rent
   b. not to pay the rent

5. **ir sin decir**:
   a. to go without saying good-bye
   b. to go without saying

6. **poderoso caballero Don Dinero**:
   a. money makes the world go 'round
   b. money is not important

7. **estar de buenas**:
   a. to be in a good mood
   b. to be in a bad mood

8. **a lo largo y a lo ancho**:
   a. throughout
   b. very tall

9. **hacer su agosto**:
   a. to make a killing
   b. to be unlucky

10. **probar fortuna**:
    a. to try one's luck
    b. to make a fortune

11. **contra viento y marea**:
    a. against the wind
    b. against all odds

12. **estar fuera de sí**:
    a. to be beside oneself
    b. to be very loud

C. Underline the appropriate word(s) that best complete(s) the phrase.

1. Seguro que el hacerse famoso se le (**bajó por la cabeza, subió a la cabeza**).

2. El dinero de la herencia me vino (**como si lloviera, como llovido del cielo**).

3. (**Por fortuna, sin fortuna**) no llovió el día de la inauguración de los Juegos Olímpicos.

4. El fin de semana pasado Juan y yo fuimos al casino a (**probar fortuna, probar una fruta**) y lo perdimos todo.

5. A Alfredo le gusta (**todo por todo, jugar el todo por el todo**); es muy arriesgado.

6. Las estrellas se extienden (**muy ancho, a lo largo y ancho**) del universo.

7. La verdad es que (**me queman las brasas, estoy en brasas**); es que muero por saber qué tal te fue el viaje.

8. (**El dinero es un caballero, Poderoso caballero Don Dinero**), ahora que es rico, todo el mundo le hace caso.

9. El pobre Carlos (**se comió una berenjena, se metió en un buen berenjenal**) cuando se mudó a esa casa tan grande.

10. Mario nunca tuvo mucho dinero; (**solía vivir al día, solía vivir al año**).

11. Rocío se enfadó tanto cuando le dieron un golpe en el coche que (**estaba en sí, estaba fuera de sí**).

12. Tuve mucha suerte, porque el Sr. Ramírez (**estaba de buenas, iba bien**) cuando me entrevistó para el trabajo.

D. CROSSWORD
Fill in the crossword puzzle on page 183 by choosing the correct word(s) from the list below.

afuera	**cielo**
agosto	**día**
ancho	**dinero**
berenjenal	**flote**
brasas	**marea**
buenas	**pie**
cabeza	**sonante**
casa	**todo**

ACROSS

12. **nacer de _____** *exp.* to be born lucky • (lit.): to be born (on foot) standing.

17. **a lo largo y a lo _____** *exp.* throughout • (lit.): lengthwise and sideways.

26. **poderoso caballero es Don _____** *exp.* money makes the world go 'round, money talks • (lit.): Mr. money is a powerful gentleman.

32. **en _____ (estar)** *exp.* to be on pins and needles, to be on tenterhooks, be uneasy • (lit.): to be in live coal.

37. **contra viento y _____** *exp.* against all odds • (lit.): against wind and tide.

41. **estar de _____** *exp.* to be in a good mood • (lit.): to be in good.

44. **_____ de sí (estar)** *exp.* beside oneself • (lit.): out of oneself.

48. **dinero contante y _____** *exp.* cold hard cash • (lit.): cash money and sounding.

53. **vivir al _____** *exp.* to live day to day, to live from hand to mouth • (lit.): to live to the day.

DOWN

7. **como llovido del _____** *exp.* like manna from heaven, heaven sent • (lit.): like rained from the sky.

10. **pagar la _____** *exp.* to pay rent • (lit.): to pay the house.

18. **subir a la _____** *exp.* to go to one's head • (lit.): to go up to one's head.

32. **meterse en un buen _____** *exp.* to get oneself into a real jam, to get oneself into a fine mess • (lit.): to get into a good eggplant patch.

33. **hacer su _____** *exp.* to make a killing • (lit.): to make one's August.

45. **ponerse a _____** *exp.* to get back up on one's own two feet again • (lit.): to put oneself afloat.

49. **jugar el _____ por el todo** *exp.* to risk everything, to go for it • (lit.): to play (risk) everything for everything.

CROSSWORD PUZZLE

E. DICTATION
Test Your Aural Comprehension

(This dictation can be found in the Appendix on page 213.)

If you are following along with your cassette, you will now hear a series of sentences from the opening dialogue. These sentences will be read by a native speaker at normal conversational speed (which may seem fast to you at first). In addition, the words will be pronounced as you would actually hear them in a conversation, often including some common reductions.

The first time the sentences are presented, simply listen in order to get accustomed to the speed and heavy use of reductions. The sentences will then be read again with a pause after each to give you time to write down what you heard. The third time the sentences are read, follow along with what you have written.

REVIEW EXAM FOR LESSONS 6-10

(Answers to Review, p. 207)

A. Underline the correct definition of the slang word(s) in boldface.

1. **llevarse como perro y gato**:
   a. to fight like cats and dogs
   b. to get along well

2. **hacer añicos**:
   a. to smash to smithereens
   b. to make new friends

3. **volver loco a uno** :
   a. to go crazy
   b. to drive someone crazy

4. **meter las narices**:
   a. to stick one's nose in
   b. to be happy

5. **por fin**:
   a. the end
   b. at last

6. **no hay ni cuatro gatos**:
   a. there's hardly a soul
   b. there are many people

7. **más vale prevenir que curar**:
   a. the more the merrier
   b. better safe than sorry

8. **estar en cueros**:
   a. to be stark-naked
   b. to be dressed up

9. **loco de remate**:
   a. intelligent
   b. crazy

10. **con el rabo del ojo**:
    a. backwards
    b. with the corner of the eye

11. **ni mucho menos**:
    b. far from it
    a. exactly

12. **de cabo a rabo**:
    a. from top to bottom
    b. from beginning to end

13. **poco a poco**:
    a. little by little
    b. less and less

14. **poner las cartas en la mesa**:
    a. to play cards
    b. to put the cards on the table

15. **a despecho**:
    a. in addition to
    b. in spite of

16. **hacer puente**:
    a. to bridge the gap
    b. to take a long weekend

17. **dentro de poco**:
    a. later
    b. any moment

18. **por lo regular**:
    a. as a general rule
    b. never

19. **de un modo u otro**:
    a. one way or another
    b. strangely

20. **cosas por el estilo**:
    a. something like that
    b. old-fashioned

21. **estar en brasas**:
    a. to be on fire
    b. to be on pins and needles

22. **no caber de contento**:
    a. to be sad
    b. to be happy

23. **poderoso caballero es Don Dinero**:
    a. money can't buy happiness
    b. money makes the world go 'round

B. Complete the following phrases by choosing the appropriate word(s) from the list below.

a toda prisa
a dos pasos de aquí
blando de corazón
en el acto
ha nacido de pie
hacer el equipaje

llevan como perro y gato
lloviendo a cántaros
meter las narices
por si acaso
por fortuna
trato hecho

1. Mi vecina es una cotilla; le gusta _____ en los asuntos de los demás.

2. Marta y María se _____; siempre están peleándose.

3. Le reconocí _____, a pesar de no haberlo visto en persona nunca.

4. La Embajada de Estados Unidos está cerquísima del hotel, sólo _____.

5. Tengo que salir _____ o llegaré tarde.

6. Ayer estuvo _____; nos tuvimos que quedar en casa todo el día.

7. _____. Tu pagas la gasolina y yo pago el automóvil.

8. No seas _____ y dile que no puedes quedarte hoy.

9. Me voy a Roma mañana, ¿quieres ayudarme a _____?

10. Voy a llevarme el abrigo _____ hace frío más tarde.

11. _____, Alberto se dio cuenta a tiempo de que casarse con ella no era lo mejor.

12. David _____, siempre encuentra trabajo.

C. Match the English phrase in the left column with the Spanish translation from the right. Mark the appropriate letter in the box.

☐ 1. If he doesn't leave once for all, he's going to drive me nuts.

☐ 2. I always like to carry some money just in case.

☐ 3. Tim and Cristina saved money for five years in order to travel around the world.

☐ 4. The weather has been lousy lately.

☐ 5. He left at full speed right after work; I didn't even have time to say goodbye to him.

☐ 6. This year it rained cats and dogs in Seville.

☐ 7. His speech didn't make any sense.

☐ 8. He discovered right away that I was telling him a lie.

☐ 9. David eats like a pig when he is really hungry.

☐ 10. He's so happy! He loves his new job.

☐ 11. I am looking for something like that.

☐ 12. This is important! Don't take this lightly.

A. Tim y Cristina estuvieron ahorrando cinco años **a fin de** hacer el viaje alrededor del mundo.

B. Este año ha **llovido a cántaros** en Sevilla.

C. ¡**No cabe de contento**! Le encanta mi nuevo trabajo.

D. Estoy buscando **algo por el estilo**.

E. Siempre me gusta llevar algo de dinero **por si acaso**.

F. Su discurso **no tuvo ni pies ni cabeza**.

G. ¡Esto es importante! **No te lo tomes a broma**.

H. Últimamente hace **un tiempo de perros**.

I. Después del trabajo salió **a toda prisa**; no tuve tiempo ni de decirle adiós.

J. David **come como un desfondado** cuando tiene mucha hambre.

K. Descubrió **en el acto** que le estaba mintiendo.

L. Como no se vaya de una vez, **me voy a volver loca**.

D. Underline the appropriate word(s) that best complete(s) the phrase.

1. Espero que solucionéis las cosas (**a despecho de**, **sin pecho de**, **despecho**) lo que os pasó.

2. A Pedro le apetece muchísimo (**equipar el equipaje**, **hacer el equipaje**, **hacer**) e irse de viaje.

3. Lo pagó todo de una vez con (**dinero y sonidos**, **dinero contante y sonante**, **sonando el dinero**)

4. El pobre Carlos (**se comió una berenjena**, **se fue con berenjenas**, **se metió en un buen berenjenal**) cuando se mudó a esa casa tan grande.

5. A Alfredo le gusta (**todo por todo**, **jugar al parchís**, **jugar el todo por el todo**); es muy arriesgado.

6. Se nota (**con las luces**, **las luces encendidas**, **a todas luces**) que le gustas mucho.

7. Creo que tienes que (**hacer frente**, **tener frente**, **estar de frente**) y sobreponerte a las circunstancias.

8. Pedro ha viajado (**a lo alto y a lo bajo**, **delgado y bajo**, **a lo largo y a lo ancho**) de este mundo.

9. Alvaro se ha vuelto (**rematadamente mal**, **loco de remate**, **remató**); de pronto se compró una moto.

10. Siempre se va solo al cine, yo (**no le bledo**, **no le importo un bledo**, **le importo bledos**).

11. Augusto siempre se va a (**dar un voltaje**, **voltear la tortilla**, **dar una vuelta**) en su moto

12. No (**te diga que es broma**, **te lo tomes a broma**, **una broma pesada**) estoy hablando muy en serio.

ANSWERS TO LESSONS 1-10

LECCIÓN UNO – ¡Me estás tomando el pelo!
(You're pulling my leg!)

Practice the Vocabulary

A.
1. ponme al corriente
2. corre el rumor
3. soy todo oídos
4. a primera vista
5. de tal palo tal astilla
6. se le cae la baba por
7. pone a todo el mundo como un trapo
8. aquí hay gato encerrado
9. tragar el anzuelo
10. tiene madera de
11. en menos que canta un gallo
12. puso el grito en el cielo

B.
1. da mala espina
2. a escondidas
3. se pasó de la raya
4. se quedó mudo
5. se le cae la baba
6. puso al corriente
7. dado gato por liebre
8. anda con rodeos
9. anda de boca en boca
10. me tomes el pelo
11. agarró / con las manos en la masa
12. a primera vista

C. 1. D   7. G
    2. C   8. H
    3. B   9. L
    4. K   10. A
    5. F   11. J
    6. E   12. I

D. **CROSSWORD PUZZLE**

LECCIÓN DOS – ¡La comida está para chuparse los dedos!
(The food is delicious!)

Practice the Vocabulary

A. 1. El pollo está para chuparse los dedos.
2. Alfonso no puede ver las mariscos ni en pintura.
3. Sobre gustos no hay nada escrito.
4. Ahora está de moda la minifalda.
5. Marta habla por los codos.
6. Eva hizo acto de presencia..
7. Jesús no entiende ni papa de inglés.
8. A David le falta un tornillo.
9. Se me hace agua la boca cuando pienso en las tortillas que hace Pepa.
10. Rafael se ahoga en un vaso de agua.

B. 1. en la punta de la lengua
2. dicen las malas lenguas
3. tiene fama de
4. llevarle la corriente
5. darle esquinazo
6. habla como un loco
7. pone en ridículo
8. entiendo ni papa
9. muy ligera de palabra
10. están de moda
11. llama la atención
12. para chuparse los dedos

C. 1. a   7. b
2. b   8. b
3. b   9. a
4. b   10. a
5. a   11. a
6. b   12. a

D. **DIALOGUE**

Ana: El año pasado estuvimos comiendo en casa de Pepa. Aún se me **hace agua la boca** pensando en lo que cocinó; todo estaba buenísimo.

Elena: Sí, ya me contaron. Por cierto, ¿**hicieron acto de presencia** los Rodríguez?

Ana: Sí, estuvieron allí con su hijo mayor ¿Cómo se llama?

Elena: Lo **tengo en la punta de la lengua**, pero no consigo acordarme.

Ana: Bueno, ya nos acordaremos.

Elena: De todas formas, él no es como su padre que **pone en ridículo** a todo el mundo contando intimidades de cada uno.

Ana: Ya, su padre es un poco **ligero de palabra.** Le gusta **llamar la atención**. Creo que en definitiva, le **falta un tornillo.**

Elena: Hablas de él como si **no pudieras verlo ni en pintura.**

Ana: Bueno, tampoco es para tanto. Sólo hay que **llevarle la corriente** y al final, es hasta gracioso.

Elena: No entiendo lo que dices. Por un lado no te gusta y por otro te parece gracioso. ¡Vaya contradicción!

Ana: Ya, **tengo fama** de contradictorio, pero en realidad es **más ruido que nueces.**

Elena: Bueno, Ana, tengo que irme, no vayan a decir **las malas lenguas** que me tomo unos descansos muy largos.

Ana: Hasta luego.

LECCIÓN TRES – Tengo que consultarlo con la almohada
(I have to sleep on it)

Practice the Vocabulary

A.
1. cortar por lo sano
2. hasta la coronilla de
3. le entra por un oído y le sale por el otro
4. uña y carne
5. consultarlo con la almohada
6. brazo derecho
7. perdí el habla
8. por las buenas o por las malas
9. hoy por hoy
10. echaba chispas
11. dar su brazo a torcer
12. hubiera estado en su pellejo

B.
1. B
2. J
3. A
4. I
5. K
6. G
7. E
8. H
9. L
10. F
11. D
12. C

C. **CROSSWORD PUZZLE**

D. 1. sin falta
    2. echo chispas
    3. echarnos un trago
    4. tan claro como el agua
    5. consulte con la almohada
    6. sudó la gota gorda
    7. cortar por lo sano
    8. por las malas o por las buenas
    9. hoy por hoy
    10. da su brazo a torcer
    11. van a echar a la calle
    12. a puerta cerrada

LECCIÓN CUATRO – ¡Tengo malas pulgas!
(I'm in a lousy mood!)

Practice the Vocabulary

A. 1. b
    2. a
    3. b
    4. a
    5. b
    6. a
    7. b
    8. b
    9. b
    10. a
    11. b
    12. a

B. 1. c
    2. c
    3. a
    4. c
    5. b
    6. a
    7. b
    8. c
    9. a
    10. c
    11. b
    12. b

C. 1. I
    2. D
    3. A
    4. K
    5. B
    6. J
    7. C
    8. E
    9. L
    10. G
    11. F
    12. H

D. **FIND-A-WORD PUZZLE**

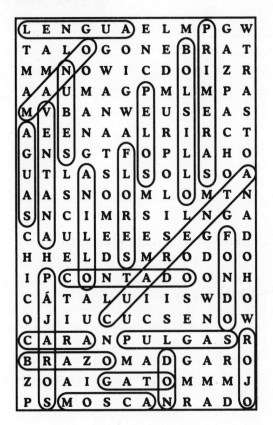

LECCIÓN CINCO – **Es un hueso duro de roer**
(She's a tough nut to crack)

Practice the Vocabulary

A.
1. con los brazos abiertos
2. misma imagen
3. hice amigo de
4. dar a luz
5. echaras una mano
6. mover un dedo
7. pierde los estribos
8. quita años
9. a pedir de boca
10. vayamos al asunto
11. salta a la vista
12. cuesta mucho trabajo

B. 1. de una vez por todas
    2. sin faltar una coma
    3. al fin y al cabo
    4. lleva los pantalones
    5. hacer un mal papel
    6. como pez en el agua
    7. hueso duro de roer
    8. dieran un portazo
    9. empezamos con buen pie
    10. como una descosida
    11. rompieron el hielo
    12. echa espumarajos

C. 1. D   5. A   9. J
    2. F   6. B   10. H
    3. I   7. K   11. C
    4. G   8. L   12. E

D. DIALOGUE

Carlos: ¿Ya conociste a tus nuevos vecinos?

Mario: Sí. Se llaman Inés y Antonio. **De una vez por todas**, decidí ir allí y **romper el hielo**. La verdad es que **empezamos con buen pie**. Me **hice amigo de** ellos en seguida. Me dieron la bienvenida **con los brazos abiertos**, no como la última señora que vivió allí. ¿Recuerdas cómo **me dio un portazo en las narices** cuando fui allí a presentarme? Verdaderamente era **un hueso duro de roer**.

Carlos: Bueno, **vayamos al asunto**. Cuéntamelo todo **sin faltar una coma**.

Mario: Bueno, al principio **me sentí como pez en el agua**. Pero entonces Inés empezó a **echar espumarajos** porque Antonio no estaba **moviendo un dedo** y ella estaba haciendo todo el trabajo de desempacar. Entonces, empezaron a **gritar como unos descosidos**. La verdad es que **perdieron los estribos**. Así que les dije que si querían que les **echara una mano**. Debo admitir que al principio **hicieron mal papel**. Pero después de unos momentos, **saltaba a la vista** que todo esto lo provocó el "stress" de estar en una casa nueva. No creo que la mudanza salió **a pedir de boca**. Pero **al fin y al cabo** todo saldrá bien.

Carlos: Así que, ¿cómo son?

Mario: Inés dice que tiene treinta años pero me **cuesta trabajo** tragármelo. Yo creo que **se quita unos años**. Yo también pienso que ella **lleva los pantalones**. Antonio **no inventó la pólvora**, pero parece ser buena persona. Ella acaba de **dar a luz** a una bebé que es la **misma imagen** que Inés.

ANSWERS TO REVIEW EXAM 1-5

A. 1. a   9. a   17. b
  2. a   10. a   18. a
  3. a   11. a   19. b
  4. b   12. b   20. b
  5. b   13. b   21. a
  6. b   14. a   22. a
  7. b   15. a   23. b
  8. b   16. a

B. 1. puso al corriente   7. tiene madera de
  2. anda de boca en boca 8. tengo en la punta de la lengua
  3. da su brazo a torcer   9. hasta la coronilla
  4. por las nubes   10. tan claro como el agua
  5. hacer un mal papel   11. mala espina
  6. hoy por hoy   12. estaba de moda

C. 1. K   7. L
  2. D   8. I
  3. G   9. E
  4. J   10. C
  5. H   11. A
  6. B   12. F

D. 1. soy todo oídos
  2. en menos que canta un gallo
  3. me dio esquinazo
  4. muy ligera de palabras
  5. pone a todo el mundo como un trapo
  6. da su brazo a torcer
  7. a puerta cerrada
  8. por las buenas o por las malas
  9. sin faltar una coma
  10. empezamos con buen pie
  11. tiene fama de
  12. Hoy por hoy

LECCIÓN SEIS – ¡Se llevan como perro y gato!
(They fight like cats and dogs!)

Practice the Vocabulary

A. 1. meter las narices
    2. volver loca
    3. hizo añicos
    4. no es cosa de juegos
    5. a todas luces
    6. de mal en peor
    7. los nervios de punta
    8. en el acto
    9. Pedro por su casa
    10. pensé para mis adentros
    11. como perro y gato
    12. romperle la crisma

B. 1. blando de corazón
    2. como desfondados
    3. estuve a dos dedos
    4. le parte el corazón
    5. mirar por mis interesas
    6. va de mal en peor
    7. pan comido
    8. pega como una ladilla
    9. me las he arreglado
    10. se llevan como perro y gato
    11. tengo los nervios de punta
    12. meter las narices

C. 1. I   7. E
    2. L   8. J
    3. H   9. D
    4. K   10. A
    5. G   11. F
    6. B   12. C

D. **CROSSWORD PUZZLE**

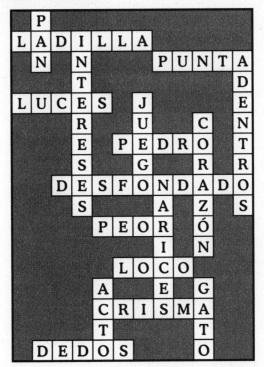

LECCIÓN SIETE – Hoy, tengo los huesos molidos
(I'm wiped out today)

Practice the Vocabulary

A.   1. b   7. a
      2. b   8. b
      3. a   9. a
      4. a   10. b
      5. b   11. a
      6. b   12. b

B. 1. a dos pasos de aquí
    2. los huesos molidos
    3. trato hecho
    4. a toda prisa
    5. loco de remate
    6. más vale prevenir que curar

    7. muero de ganas
    8. la carne de gallina
    9. lloviendo a cántaros
    10. había ni cuatro gatos
    11. hizo furor
    12. a dar una vuelta

C. 1. G
    2. H
    3. J
    4. A
    5. K
    6. I

    7. C
    8. D
    9. L
    10. B
    11. E
    12. F

D. **FIND-A-WORD PUZZLE**

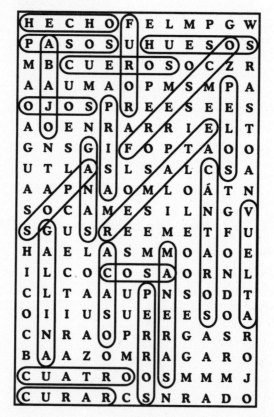

LECCIÓN OCHO – ¡Lo mandé a bañar!
(I told him to go take a flying leap!)

Practice the Vocabulary

A. 1. b
    2. a
    3. a
    4. b
    5. b
    6. a
    7. a
    8. a
    9. a
    10. b
    11. a
    12. b

B. 1. un humor de perros
    2. cuestan un ojo de la cara
    3. pon las cartas sobre la mesa
    4. no quiero nada que ver
    5. de cabo a rabo
    6. hacer las paces
    7. ni mucho menos
    8. poco a poco
    9. da en el clavo
    10. no puedo más
    11. hacer el equipaje
    12. ponme al corriente

C. 1. costando un ojo de la cara
    2. de cabo a rabo
    3. no puedo más
    4. no le importo un bledo
    5. a despecho de
    6. hacer el equipaje
    7. la gota que derramó el vaso
    8. ponerte al corriente
    9. ni mucho menos
    10. a medias
    11. de un humor de perros
    12. hacer puente

D. **DIALOGUE**

Vivian: ¿Te has enterado de lo que ha ocurrido en Badajoz?

Liliana: No, **ponme al corriente.** Cuéntame todo **de cabo a rabo**.

Vivian: Hace unos días hubo una tormenta terrible; trece muertos en total. Pero **la gota que derramó el vaso** es el hecho de que la catástrofe ocurrió en un barrio obrero, que no contaba con la infraestructura adecuada. Como comprenderás la gente está **de un humor de perros.**

Liliana: ¿Por qué? ¿Hay responsables?

Vivian: Bueno, en realidad es posible que los haya, pues se trata de una comunidad **escasa de fondos,** y el ayuntamiento encima no ha hecho nada al respecto. Creo que el alcalde va a tener que **hacer el equipaje** y largarse. El gobierno local y el central se han comprometido a **ir a medias** en las reparaciones. En estos momentos, el presidente **está a punto de hacer** unas declaraciones al respecto. Creo que les va **a costar un ojo de la cara** volver a la normalidad.

Liliana: ¡Qué horror! Además, esa zona es bastante seca y no están nada preparados para estas situaciones. Espero que **poco a poco** todo se resuelva.

Vivian: Sí, alguien va a tener que **hacer frente** a la situación; la gente **no puede más**.

LECCIÓN NUEVE – ¡Ricardo me ha dejado plantada!
(Richard stood me up!)

Practice the Vocabulary

A. 1. a   5. b   9. a
    2. b   6. a   10. a
    3. a   7. a   11. b
    4. b   8. a   12. a

B.
1. no tiene ni pies ni cabeza
2. no tiene ni un pelo de tonta
3. hasta la fecha
4. a fin de
5. así, así
6. hacer frente al hecho de
7. a toda prisa
8. me ha dejado plantado
9. por lo general
10. ya es harina de otro costal
11. da tanta rabia
12. por ningún motivo

C.
1. H
2. K
3. A
4. G
5. B
6. L
7. C
8. J
9. E
10. I
11. D
12. F

D. **FIND-A-WORD CUBE**

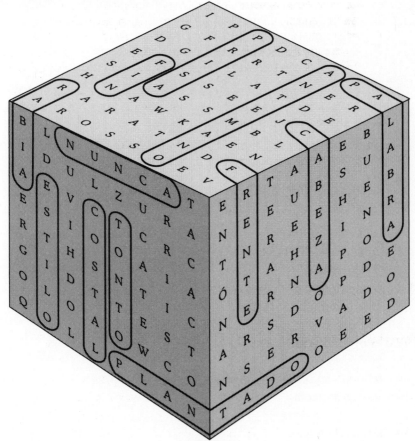

LECCIÓN DIEZ – ¡Se metió en un buen berenjenal!
(He got himself into a real jam!)

Practice the Vocabulary

A. 1. probé fortuna
    2. sube a la cabeza
    3. contra viento y marea
    4. como llovida del cielo
    5. hizo su agosto
    6. a lo largo y ancho
    7. jugó el todo por el todo
    8. metimos en un buen berenjenal
    9. nacido de pie
   10. dinero contante y sonante
   11. está de buenas
   12. por fortuna

B. 1. a   7. a
    2. b   8. a
    3. b   9. a
    4. a   10. a
    5. b   11. a
    6. a   12. b

C. 1. subió a la cabeza
    2. como llovido del cielo
    3. Por fortuna
    4. probar fortuna
    5. jugar el todo por el todo
    6. a lo largo y ancho
    7. estoy en brasas
    8. poderoso caballero Don Dinero
    9. se metió en un buen berenjenal
   10. solía vivir al día
   11. estaba fuera de sí
   12. estaba de buenas

D. **CROSSWORD PUZZLE**

ANSWERS TO REVIEW EXAM 6-10

A. 1. a
    2. a
    3. b
    4. a
    5. b
    6. a
    7. b
    8. a
    9. b
    10. b
    11. b
    12. b
    13. a
    14. b
    15. b
    16. b
    17. b
    18. a
    19. a
    20. a
    21. b
    22. b
    23. b

B.　1.　meter las narices
　　2.　llevan como perro y gato
　　3.　en el acto
　　4.　a dos pasos de aquí
　　5.　a toda prisa
　　6.　lloviendo a cántaros
　　7.　trato hecho
　　8.　blando de corazón
　　9.　hacer el equipaje
　10.　por si acaso
　11.　por fortuna
　12.　ha nacido de pie

C.　1.　L
　　2.　E
　　3.　A
　　4.　H
　　5.　I
　　6.　B
　　7.　F
　　8.　K
　　9.　J
　10.　C
　11.　D
　12.　G

D.　1.　a despecho
　　2.　hacer el equipaje
　　3.　dinero contante y sonante
　　4.　se metió en un buen berenjenal
　　5.　jugar el todo por el todo
　　6.　a todas luces
　　7.　hacer frente
　　8.　a lo largo y a lo ancho
　　9.　loco de remate
　10.　no le importo un bledo
　11.　dar una vuelta
　12.　te lo tomes a broma

APPENDIX
-Dictations-

¡Me estás tomando el pelo!
(You're pulling my leg!)

1. Bueno, te voy a **poner al corriente**.
2. No quiero **correr el rumor**, pero **anda de boca en boca**.
3. Soy **todo oídos**.
4. ¡Me **estás tomando el pelo**!
5. ¡Me he **quedado muda**!
6. **De tal palo tal astilla**.
7. Mark **tenía madera** para ser un buen marido.
8. **El hábito no hace al monje**.

Lección Dos

¡La comida está para chuparse los dedos!
(The food is delicious!)

1. La comida parece **para chuparse los dedos**.
2. ¡Se me está **haciendo agua la boca**!
3. **Lo tengo en la punta de la lengua**.
4. Se está **poniendo en ridículo** ella misma.
5. Yo le voy a **llevar la corriente**.
6. Vamos a **darle esquinazo**.
7. Tú ya sabes que es **muy ligera de palabra**.
8. ¡Algunas veces **no entiendo ni papa**!

Lección Tres

Tengo que consultarlo con la almohada
(I have to sleep on it)

1. Marco y el jefe han estado **a puerta cerrada** varias horas.

2. Finalmente ha decidido **echar a la calle** a Marco.

3. **Del dicho al hecho hay mucho trecho**.

4. No solo ha sido **su brazo derecho**, sino también es su amigo.

5. **Está tan claro como el agua**.

6. El Jefe estaba **echando chispas**.

7. He **perdido el habla**.

8. Me alegro de no **estar en su pellejo**.

Lección Cuatro

¡Tengo malas pulgas!
(I'm in a lousy mood!)

1. Los precios aquí **están por las nubes**.

2. Te sienta **como anillo al dedo**.

3. Te lo **digo con el corazón en la mano**, estás guapísima.

4. Si no dejas de **echarme flores**, ¡me voy a **poner colorada**!

5. Me has **torcido el brazo**.

6. ¡Tampoco tienes que **echar la casa por la ventana**!

7. Desde luego **no tiene pelos en la lengua**.

8. Siempre **tiene malas pulgas**.

Lección Cinco

Es un hueso duro de roer
(She's a tough nut to crack)

1. **De una vez por todas**, decidí ir allí y **romper el hielo**.

2. La verdad es que **empezamos con buen pie**.

3. Me **hice amigo de** ellos en seguida.

4. Era **un hueso duro de roer**.

5. Bueno, **vayamos al asunto**.

6. Cuéntamelo todo **sin faltar una coma**.

7. Inés empezó a **echar espumarajos**.

8. Empezaron a **gritar como unos desconocidos**.

Lección Seis

¡Se llevan como perro y gato!
(They fight like cats and dogs!)

1. La situación va **de mal en peor**.

2. Se me **pega como una ladilla**.

3. **Come como un desfondado**.

4. Estoy **a dos dedos** de gritar.

5. ¡Tengo ganas de **romperle la crisma**!

6. **No es cosa de juego**.

7. ¡Tengo **los nervios de punta**!

8. Va a ser **pan comido**.

Lección Siete

Hoy, tengo los huesos molidos
(I'm wiped out today)

1. Vamos a **dar una vuelta** por el parque.

2. ¡**Trato hecho**!

3. Me encantaría **tomar un poco de aire fresco**.

4. Será divertido **clavarle los ojos** a toda la gente.

5. ¡**No hay ni cuatro gatos** aquí!

6. Yo **tenía los huesos molidos**.

7. Me **dormí a fondo boca abajo**.

8. ¡Qué **tiempo de perros**!

Lección Ocho

¡Lo mandé a bañar!
(I told him to go take a flying leap!)

1. Así que **ponme al día**.

2. Fue horrible **de cabo a rabo**.

3. Estuve **a punto** de **hacer el equipaje**.

4. ¡**No quiero tener nada que ver** con él otra vez!

5. Ramón estaba siempre **de un humor de perros**.

6. Estas vacaciones me **costaron un ojo de la cara**.

7. ¡Has **dado en el clavo**!

8. Tenía tantas ganas de **hacer puente**.

Lección Nueve

¡Ricardo me ha dejado plantada!
(Ricardo stood me up!)

1. ¡Ricardo **me ha dejado plantada**!

2. ¡Los hombres me **dan tanta rabia**!

3. ¡Eso **no tiene ni pies ni cabeza**!

4. ¡No te lo **tomes a broma**!

5. Yo **no tengo ni un pelo de tonta**.

6. ¿Por qué no le puedes **tomar la palabra**?

7. Eso es **harina de otro costal**.

8. ¡**Más vale tarde que nunca**!

Lección Diez

¡Se metió en un buen berenjenal!
(He got himself into a real jam!)

1. Estoy **en brasas**.

2. ¡**Hizo su agosto**!

3. Le vino **como llovido del cielo**.

4. **Se metió en un buen berenjenal**.

5. Casi no podía **pagar la casa**.

6. Ahora va a poder **ponerse a flote** otra vez.

7. Debe de estar **afuera de sí**.

8. Se va a comprar un automóvil con **dinero contante y sonante**!

GLOSSARY

a decir verdad *exp.* to tell you the truth • (lit.): to tell truth.
example: **A decir verdad**, te quiero mucho.
translation: **To tell you the truth**, I love you very much.

a despecho de *exp.* in spite of • (lit.): to spite of.
example: Bueno **a despecho de** lo que pasó espero que sigamos siendo amigos.
translation: Well, **in spite of** what happened I hope we are still friends.

a dos dedos de (estar) *exp.* to be on the verge of • (lit.): to be two fingers from.
example: Estoy **a dos dedos de** comprar una casa.
translation: I'm **on the verge of** buying a house.

a dos pasos de aquí *exp.* nearby, a hop, skip, and a jump from here • (lit.): two steps from here.
example: La casa de Laura está **a dos pasos de** aquí.
translation: Laura's house is **a hop, skip, and a jump** from here.
ANTONYM: en el quinto pino *exp.* very far away • (lit.): in the fifth pine tree.

a escondidas *exp.* secretly, on the sly • (lit.): on the hiding [from the verb esconder meaning "to hide"].
example: Pablo y Sonia fueron al cine **a escondidas**.
translation: Pablo and Sonia went to the movies **secretly**.

a fin de *exp.* in order to • (lit.): to end of.
example: Voy a comer menos **a fin de** perder peso.
translation: I'm going to eat less **in order to** lose weight.
SYNONYM: con el fin de *exp.* • (lit.): with the end of.

a lo largo y a lo ancho *exp.* throughout • (lit.): lengthwise and sideways.
example: Manuel siempre ha tenido mucha suerte **a lo largo y a lo ancho** de su vida.
translation: Manuel's always been very lucky **throughout** his life.

a pedir de boca *exp.* smoothly • (lit.): to taste from the mouth.
example: Esta presentación me ha salido **a pedir de boca**.
translation: This presentation **went smoothly**.
NOTE: This popular expression can also be used in the culinary world when a dish has been prepared to perfection meaning "delicious" or "perfect" • *Esta langosta está a pedir de boca;* This lobster is delicious.

a primera vista *exp.* at first glance • (lit.): at first look.

example: **A primera vista**, Manolo parece buena persona.

translation: **At first glance**, Manolo seems like a nice guy.

a puerta cerrada *exp.* behind closed doors • (lit.): at closed door.

example: Los ejecutivos de la empresa tuvieron una reunión **a puerta cerrada**.

translation: The company's executives had a meeting **behind closed doors**.

SYNONYM -1: en clausura *exp.* • (lit.): in confinement (said of life in a monastery).

SYNONYM -2: en privado *exp.* • (lit.): in private.

ANTONYM: a puerta abierta *exp.* with opened doors • (lit.): at opened door.

a punto de *exp.* on the point of; on the verge of, about to • (lit.): at point of.

example: Estuve **a punto de** decirle lo que pienso de él.

translation: I was **on the verge of** telling him what I think about him.

a toda prisa *exp.* at full speed, as quickly as possible • (lit.): at all speed.

example: Salí de mi casa **a toda prisa** cuando me enteré de la emergencia.

translation: I left my house **as quickly as possible** when I heard about the emergency.

SYNONYM -1: a toda vela *exp.* • (lit.): at all sail.

SYNONYM -2: en menos que canta un gallo *exp.* • (lit.): in less time than a hen can sing.

SYNONYM -3: en un avemaría *exp.* • (lit.): in one Hail Mary.

SYNONYM -4: en un periquete *exp.* (Southern Spain).

a toda prisa *exp.* at full speed, as quickly as possible • (lit.): at all speed.

example: Voy a la escuela **a toda prisa** porque me levanté tarde.

translation: I'm going to school **at full speed** because I woke up late.

SYNONYM -1: a toda vela *exp.* • (lit.): at all sail.

SYNONYM -2: a todo meter *exp.* (Southern Spain) • (lit.): at all introduce.

SYNONYM -3: en un avemaría *exp.* • (lit.): in one Hail Mary.

SYNONYM -4: en un chiflido *exp.* • (lit.): in one whistle.

SYNONYM -5: en un credo *exp.* • (lit.): in one creed.

SYNONYM -6: en un decir Jesús *exp.* • (lit.): in one saying of Jesus.

SYNONYM -7: en un dos por tres *exp.* • (lit.): in a two by three.

SYNONYM -8: en un improviso *exp.* (Colombia, Venezuela, Mexico) • (lit.): in one sudden action.

SYNONYM -9: en un salto *exp.* • (lit.): in one leap.

SYNONYM -10: en un soplo *exp.* • (lit.): in a gust or blow.

a todas luces *exp.* any way you look at it, clearly • (lit.): by all lights.

example: Se ve que tiene dinero **a todas luces**.

translation: You can **clearly** tell he's got money.

SYNONYM: a toda luz *exp.* • (lit.): by all light.

NOTE: This could best be compared to the American expression, "the lights are on but nobody's home."

afuera de sí (estar) *exp.* beside oneself • (lit.): out of oneself.

example: Alberto parece **estar afuera de sí**. Que pasó?

translation: Alberto seems **to be beside himself**. What happened?

SYNONYM: **fuera de sí** *exp.* • (lit.): out of oneself.

agarrar con las manos en la masa *exp.* to catch [someone] red-handed, to catch [someone] in the act • (lit.): to catch [someone] with the hands in the dough.

example: A Luis lo **agarraron con las manos en la masa** cuando pretendía robar un carro.

translation: Luis was **caught red-handed** when he was trying to steal a car.

SYNONYM -1: **coger con las manos en la masa** *exp. (Spain)* • (lit.): to catch [someone] with his/her hands in the dough.

SYNONYM -2: **coger/agarrar/ atrapar en el acto** *exp.* • (lit.): to catch [someone] in the act.

SYNONYM -3: **coger/agarrar/ atrapar en plena acción** *exp.* • (lit.): to catch [someone] right in the action.

NOTE: In these types of expressions, the verb *coger* is used primarily in Spain. In the rest of the Spanish-speaking world, agarrar and atrapar are most commonly used.

ahogarse en un vaso de agua *exp.* to get all worked up about something, to make a mountain out of a molehill • (lit.): to drown in a glass of water.

example: Antonio se preocupa demasiado de todo. Siempre **se ahoga en un vaso de agua**.

translation: Antonio worries too much about everything. He always **makes a mountain out of a molehill**.

SYNONYM: **ahogarse en poca agua** *exp.* • (lit.): to drown (oneself) in little water.

al fin y al cabo *exp.* after all, when the dust clears • (lit.): to the end and to the end.

example: **Al fin y al cabo** todo salió bien.

translation: **When all was said and done**, everything turned out okay.

algo por el estilo *exp.* something like that, similar. • (lit.): something of the same style.

example: Esa casa es **algo por el estilo** a la mía.

translation: That house **is similar** to mine.

SYNONYM: **cosas por el estilo** *exp.* • (lit.): things of the same style.

andar con rodeos *exp.* to beat around the bush • (lit.): to walk with detours.

example: Alfredo siempre **anda con rodeos** cuando quiere explicar algún problema.

translation: Alfredo always **beats around the bush** when he wants to explain a problem.

SYNONYM: **andarse por las ramas** *exp.* • (lit.): to stroll/walk by the branches.

NOTE: **emborrachar la perdiz** *exp. (Chile)* to beat around the bush • (lit.): to get the partridge drunk.

andar de boca en boca *exp.* to be generally known, to be in everyone's lips, to have everyone talking about it • (lit.): to walk from mouth to mouth.

example: **Anda de boca en boca** que José se va a casar con Rocio.

translation: **Everyone's talking about** José marrying Rocio.

SYNONYM -1: **andar en boca de las gentes** *exp.* • (lit.): to walk on people's mouths.

SYNONYM -2: **andar en boca de todos** *exp.* • (lit.): to walk in everyone's mouth.

arreglárselas para *exp.* to manage to • (lit.): to arrange oneself by.

example: No puedo **arreglármelas para** levantar esta caja. ¿Me puedes ayudar?

translation: I can't **manage to** lift this heavy box. Can you help me?

así, así *exp.* so, so • (lit.): such, such.

example: ¿Te gustan las películas de miedo? **Así, así**.

translation: Do you like horror movies? **So, so**.

B

blando/a de corazón (ser) *exp.* to be soft-hearted • (lit.): to be soft of heart.

example: Marcos es muy **blando de corazón**.

translation: Marcos is very **soft-hearted**.

ANTONYM -1: **corazón de piedra (tener)** *exp.* to be very hardhearted • (lit.): to have a heart made of stone.

ANTONYM -2: **duro/a de corazón (ser)** *exp.* to be hard-hearted • (lit.): to be hard of heart.

buscarle tres pies al gato *exp.* to go looking for trouble • (lit.): to look for three of the cat's feet.

example: ¡Relájate! No le **busques tres pies al gato**.

translation: Relax! Don't **look for trouble**.

SYNONYM -1: **buscarle cinco pies al gato** *exp.* • (lit.): to look for five of the cat's feet.

SYNONYM -2: **buscarle mangas al chaleco** *exp.* • (lit.): to look for sleeves in the vest.

NOTE: **buscarle los tres pies al gato** *exp.* (Cuba) It's interesting to note that in Cuba, the definite article los is used before tres pies.

C

caérsele la baba por *exp.* to be wild about, to love someone • (lit.): to slobber for.

example: A Marcos **se le cae la baba por** Patricia.

translation: Marcos **is wild about** Patricia.

cantarle las cuarenta *exp.* to tell someone off • (lit.): to sing the forty (truths about the person).

example: ¡Estoy harto! ¡Voy a **cantarle las cuarenta**!

translation: I'm fed up! I'm going **to tell him off**!

cara a cara *exp.* **1.** right to a person's face • **2.** privately • (lit.): face to face.

example: Me gustaría hablar con Jaime **cara a cara**.

translation: I would like to talk to Jaime **privately**.

SYNONYM: **frente a frente** *exp.* • (lit.): front to front.

carne de gallina *exp.* goose bumps
• (lit.): chicken meat.
example: Se me puso **la carne de gallina** cuando oí las noticias.
translation: I got **goose bumps** when I heard the news.

clavar los ojos a/en *exp.* to stare at, to fix one's eyes on, to check out • (lit.): to nail one's eyes on.
example: No puedo dejar de **clavarle los ojos a** este cuadro. ¡Es precioso!
translation: I can't stop **staring at** that painting. It's beautiful!
SYNONYM -1: **clavar la atención en** *exp.* • (lit.): to fix one's attention on.
SYNONYM -2: **clavar la vista en** *exp.* • (lit.): to nail the sight on.
SYNONYM -3: **hacer ojitos** *exp.* (Mexico & some regions of Spain) • (lit.): to make little eyes.
SYNONYM -4: **hacer ojos** *exp.* (Colombia) • (lit.): to make eyes.

comer como un desfondado *exp.* to eat like a pig • (lit.): to eat like someone without a bottom (to eat like a bottomless pit).
example: Jorge está tan gordo porque siempre **come como un desfondado**.
translation: Jorge is so fat because he always **eats like a pig**.
SYNONYM -1: **comer como si fuera la última cena** *exp.* • (lit.): to eat as if it were the last supper.
SYNONYM -2: **comer como si no hubiera comido nunca** *exp.* • (lit.): to eat as if one never ate before.
NOTE: The noun *desfondado* comes from the verb desfondar meaning "to go through" or "to break the bottom of."

como anillo al dedo (quedar) *exp.* to fit to a T • (lit.): to fit like a ring to a finger.

example: Ese vestido te queda **como anillo al dedo**.
translation: That dress **fits you to a T**.
SYNONYM: **sentar de maravilla** *exp.* • (lit.): to feel wonderful.

como llovido del cielo *exp.* like manna from heaven, heaven sent • (lit.): like rained from the sky.
example: Ese dinero me vino **como llovido del cielo**.
translation: That money came **like manna from heaven**.

como Pedro por su casa *exp.* to feel right at home, to act like one owns the place • (lit.): like Pedro in his house.
example: Juan siempre anda en la oficina **como Pedro por su casa**.
translation: Juan always walks around the office **as if he owned the place**.

como pez en el agua (sentirse) *exp.* to feel right at home • (lit.): to feel like a fish in water.
example: Estoy muy contento. **Me siento como pez en el agua**.
translation: I'm so happy. **I feel right at home**.
SYNONYM: **como Pedro por su casa (andar)** *exp.* • (lit.): like Pedro in his house.
ANTONYM -1: **como [un] pez fuera del agua (estar)** *exp.* to feel out of place, to feel like a fish out of water • (lit.): to be like a fish out of water.
ANTONYM -2: **como gallina en corral ajeno (estar)** *exp.* • (lit.): to be like a chicken in a strange pen.
ANTONYM -3: **como perro en barrio ajeno (estar)** *exp.* • (lit.): to be like a dog in a strange neighborhood.

con el corazón en la mano *exp.*
in all frankness, in all honesty • (lit.):
with the heart in the hand.
example: Te lo digo **con el corazón
en la mano**. Yo creo que eres muy
guapa.
translation: I'm telling you **in all
honesty**. I think that you're beautiful.

con los brazos abiertos *exp.* with
open arms.
example: Cuando Juan volvió de la
guerra, le recibimos **con los brazos
abiertos**.
translation: When Juan came back from
the war, we welcomed him **with
open arms**.

consultarlo con la almohada
exp. to sleep on eat • (lit.): to consult it
with the pillow.
example: Esa decisión tan importante,
tendré que **consultarla con la
almohada**.
translation: It's such a big decision, I will
have **to sleep on it**.

contra viento y marea *exp.*
against all odds • (lit.): against wind
and tide.
example: La tortuga ganó la carrera
contra viento y marea.
translation: The tortoise won the race
against all odds.

correr el rumor *exp.* to be rumored
• (lit.): to run the rumor.
example: **Corre el rumor** que
mañana van a despedir a Carlos.
translation: **It's been rumored** that
Carlos is going to get fired tomorrow.

cortar por lo sano *exp.* to take
drastic measures • (lit.): to cut
(something off) and leave only the
healthy parts.
example: Voy a **cortar por los sano**
y empezar de nuevo.

translation: I'm going **to take
drastic measures** and start all over
again.

cosa de *exp.* approximately, about,
more or less • (lit.): thing of.
example: Vuelvo en **cosa de** dos
horas.
translation: I'll be back **in
approximately** two hours.
NOTE: ser cosas de... *exp.* to be
the way ... is • (lit.): to be things of •
Esas son cosas de Javier; That's just
the way Javier is.

costar trabajo hacer algo *exp.*
to have trouble believing/ swallowing
something • (lit.): to cost work.
example: **Me cuesta trabajo** creer
que Pedro ganó la apuesta.
translation: **I have trouble** believing
that Pedro won the bet.

costar un ojo de la cara *exp.* to
cost an arm and a leg • (lit.): to cost
an eye from the face.
example: Ese abrigo **me costó un
ojo de la cara**.
translation: That coat **cost me an
arm and a leg**.
SYNONYM -1: costar un huevo
exp. (Venezuela, Colombia, Bolivia,
Ecuador, Peru, Spain) • (lit.): to cost
an egg.
NOTE: This common expression is
somewhat rude since the masculine
noun "huevo" is commonly used to
mean "testicle" in many Spanish-
speaking countries.
**SYNONYM -2: costar un huevo
y medio** *exp.* • (lit.): to cost an egg
and a half.
NOTE: This is a variation of the
previous expression and is equally
common.

cuando más *exp.* at most • (lit.):
when more.

example: Javier debe tener 18 años **cuando más**.

translation: Javier must be 18 years old **at most**.

NOTE: This common expression is used primarily in Latin- American countries. • (lit.): when more.

ANTONYM: **cuando menos** exp. at least • (lit.): when less.

dar [tanta] rabia exp. to make one [so] mad • (lit.): to give rage.

example: **Me da tanta rabia** cuando la gente llega tarde a una cita.

translation: **It gets me so ticked off** when people arrive late to an appointment.

dar a luz a exp. to give birth to • (lit.): to give light to.

example: Marta **dio a luz a** una preciosa niña.

translation: Marta **gave birth to a** beautiful girl.

dar en el clavo exp. to hit the nail on the head, to put one's finger on it • (lit.): to hit on the nail.

example: ¡Tienes razón! ¡Has **dado en el clavo**!

translation: You're right! You just **hit the nail on the head**!

SYNONYM: **dar el hito** exp. • (lit.): to hit on the stone.

NOTE -1: **dar en** exp. to hit on • (lit.): to give on.

NOTE -2: **dar con (algo)** exp. to find (something) • (lit.): to give with.

dar esquinazo exp. to avoid [someone], to ditch someone • (lit.): to give [someone] a corner.

example: ¡Vamos a **darle esquinazo** a Julio! Es un pesado.

translation: Let's **ditch** Julio! He's so annoying.

dar gato por liebre exp. to pull the wool over someone's eyes • (lit.): to give a cat instead of a hare.

example: **Le dieron gato por liebre** cuando Jorge compró esa casa. Tenía muchos problemas de plomería.

translation: They **pulled the wool over his eyes** when Jorge bought that house. It was full of plumbing problems.

dar mala espina exp. to arouse one's suspicions • (lit.): to give a bad thorn.

example: A Mario **le dio mala espina** cuando vio a una persona salir del banco corriendo.

translation: It **aroused** Mario's **suspicions** when he saw a person running out of the bank.

dar un portazo exp. to slam the door • (lit.): to give a slam (of a door).

example: ¡No **des portazos** por favor!

translation: Please don't **slam the door**!

SYNONYM: **tirar la puerta** exp. • (lit.): to throw the door.

dar una vuelta exp. to take a stroll, a walk • (lit.): to give a turn.

example: Hace un día muy bonito. Vamos a **dar una vuelta**.

translation: It's a beautiful day. Let's **go for a stroll**.

SYNONYM -1: **dar un paseo** exp. • (lit.): to give a passage.

SYNONYM -2: pasear a pie *exp.* •
(lit.): to walk by foot.
SYNONYM -3: tomar el aire *exp.* •
(lit.): to take the air.

de antemano *exp.* ahead of time •
(lit.): of beforehand.
example: Yo siempre llego a mi trabajo
de antemano.
translation: I always arrive at my work
ahead of time.

de buenas a primeras *exp.*
suddenly (and unexpectedly), right off
the bat, from the very start • (lit.): from
the good ones to the first ones.
example: Ana me dijo que no quería
salir más conmigo **de buenas a
primeras**.
translation: Ana told me **right off the
bat** she didn't want to go out with me
anymore.
SYNONYM -1: de repente *exp.* •
(lit.): suddenly (of sudden movement).
SYNONYM -2: luego, luego *adv.*
(Mexico) right away • (lit.): later, later.
NOTE: Although its literal translation
is indeed "later, later," when *luego* is
repeated twice, it means, oddly
enough, "right away, immediately."

NOTE: This could be compared to
the American expression "to have a
real good cold" where "real good"
actually refers to something that is
negative or unpleasant.

de cabo a rabo *exp.* from beginning
to end • (lit.): from end to tail.
example: Me leí "El Quijote" **de cabo a
rabo**.
translation: I read "Don Quixote" **from
beginning to end**.
SYNONYM -1: de cabo a cabo *exp.*
• (lit.): from end to end.
SYNONYM -2: de punta a punta
exp. • (lit.): from point to point.

de mal en peor (ir) *exp.* to go
from bad to worse • (lit.): [same].
example: Las cosas van **de mal en
peor** entre Fernando y Verónica.
translation: Things are going **from
bad to worse** between Fernando
and Veronica.

de moda (estar) *exp.* to be
fashionable, to be chic, to be in style •
(lit.): to be of fashion.
example: Verónica siempre **se viste
de moda**.
translation: Verónica always **dresses
in style**.
SYNONYM: de buen tono *exp.* •
(lit.): of good tone.
VARIATION: a la moda (estar)
exp. • (lit.): of good tone.

de tal palo tal astilla *exp.* like
father like son, a chip off the old block
• (lit.): from such stick comes such
splinter.
example: Alvaro quiere ser policía
como su papá. **De tal palo tal
astilla**.
translation: Alvaro wants to become a
policeman like his dad. **Like father
like son**.

de todas maneras *exp.* at any rate,
in any case • (lit.): in all manners.
example: No puedo creerme cuánto
trabajo tengo. **De todas maneras**,
me voy a Inglaterra por la mañana.
translation: I can't believe how much
work I have to do. **At any rate**, I'm
leaving for England in the morning.
SYNONYM: de todos modos *exp.*
• (lit.): in all modes.

**de un humor de perros
(estar)** *exp.* to be in a lousy mood •
(lit.): to be in a mood of dogs.
example: ¡**Estoy de un humor de
perros** porque alguien me robó mi
bicicleta!

translation: **I'm in a lousy mood** because someone stole my bicycle today!

SYNONYM: **tener malas pulgas** *exp.* • (lit.): to have bad fleas.

NOTE: The expression *de perros* meaning "lousy" can be used to modify other nouns as well. A variation of *de perros* is *perro/a*. For example: Pasé una noche perra; I had a hell of a night.

de un modo u otro *exp.* one way or another • (lit.): of a way or another
example: **De un modo u otro** iré a visitarte este verano.
translation: **One way or another** I'll visit you next summer.

de una vez por todas *exp.* once and for all • (lit.): for one time and for all.
example: Voy a terminar este proyecto **de una vez por todas**.
translation: I'm going to finish this project **once and for all**.

SYNONYM -1: **de una vez** *exp.* • (lit.): for one time.

SYNONYM -2: **de una vez y para siempre** *exp.* • (lit.): for one time and for always.

dejar plantado/a a alguien *exp.* to stand someone up, to leave in the lurch • (lit.): to leave someone planted.
example: ¡No lo puedo creer! ¡Verónica **me dejó plantado**!
translation: I can't believe it! Veronica **stood me up**!

del dicho al hecho hay mucho trecho *exp.* easier said than done • (lit.): from what someone says to the facts, there's a long way to go.
example: Tienes que despedir a Juan, pero **del dicho al hecho hay mucho trecho**. Es tu mejor amigo.

translation: You have to fire Juan, but **it's easier said than done**. He's your best friend.

dentro de poco *exp.* any moment, soon • (lit.): in a little bit.
example: Carlos llegará **dentro de poco**.
translation: Carlos will arrive **any moment**.

dinero contante y sonante *exp.* cold hard cash • (lit.): cash money and sounding.
example: Alfonso pagó su casa con **dinero contante y sonante**.
translation: Alfonso paid for his house with **cold hard cash**.

SYNONYM -1: **dinero al contado** *exp.* • (lit.): counting money.

SYNONYM -2: **dinero en efectivo** *exp.* • (lit.): effective money.

dormir [a fondo] boca abajo *exp.* to sleep on one's stomach • (lit.): to sleep [deeply] with the mouth under.
example: Desde que Estefanía se dañó la espalda, solo puede **dormir a fondo boca abajo**.
translation: Ever since Estefanía hurt her back, she can only **sleep on her stomach**.

SYNONYM: **dormir a pata suelta** *exp.* • (lit.): to sleep with a lose leg.

echar a alguien a la calle *exp.* to fire someone, to can someone • (lit.): to throw someone to the street.

example: Parece que a Tomás lo **echaron a la calle** porque siempre llegaba tarde al trabajo.

translation: It looks like they **fired** Tomas because he was always late to work.

SYNONYM -1: **arrojar a la calle** *exp.* • (lit.): to throw [someone/ something] to the street.

SYNONYM -2: **correr** *v. (Mexico).* • (lit.): to run.

SYNONYM -3: **despedir** *v.* • (lit.): to say goodbye to.

echar chispas *exp.* to be furious, to be mad or angry • (lit.): to throw sparks.

example: El jefe estaba **echando chispas** cuando se enteró que Andrés llamó enfermo tres veces esta semana.

translation: The boss **was furious** when he found out Andres called in sick for the third time this week.

SYNONYM -1: **echar fuego por las orejas** *exp.* • (lit.): to throw fire through the ears.

echar espumarajos [por la boca] *exp.* to be furious, to foam at the mouth with rage • (lit.): to throw foam [from the mouth].

example: Rafael está **echando espumarajos [por la boca]** porque le robaron su coche.

translation: Rafael is furious **because somebody stole his car.**

SYNONYM -1: **echar humo** *exp.* • (lit.): to throw smoke (in the air).

SYNONYM -2: **enchilarse** *v.* (Mexico) • (lit.): to get red in the face from eating chilies.

echar flores [a alguien] *exp.* to flatter [someone], to butter [someone] up • (lit.): to throw flowers at someone.

example: No le **eches flores** a Ramón. No va a cambiar de opinión.

translation: Don't **flatter** Ramón. He's not going to change his mind.

SYNONYM -1: **darle la suave a uno** *exp.* (Mexico) • (lit.): to give the soft to someone.

SYNONYM -2: **pasar la mano por el lomo** *exp.* • (lit.): to pass the hand by the back (of an animal).

SYNONYM -3: **pasarle la mano a alguien** *exp.* • (lit.): to pass one's hand to someone.

echar una mano a alguien *exp.* to lend someone a hand • (lit.): to throw someone a hand.

example: Voy a **echarle una mano** a Juan con esas cajas.

translation: I'm going **to lend** Juan **a hand** Juan with those boxes.

SYNONYM -1: **dar una mano a alguien** *exp.* • (lit.): to give someone a hand.

SYNONYM -2: **echar la mano a alguien** *exp.* • (lit.): to throw the hand to someone.

echar/tirar la casa por la ventana *exp.* to go overboard • (lit.): to throw the house out the window.

example: ¿Viste cómo Cristina decoró su nueva casa? La verdad es que esta vez **echó la casa por la ventana**.

translation: Did you see how Cristina decorated her new house? She really **went overboard**.

echarse un trago *exp.* to have a drink • (lit.): to throw a swallow.

example: A mi papá le gusta **echarse un trago** después del trabajo.

translation: My father likes **to have a drink** after work.

NOTE: The verb *tragar*, literally meaning "to swallow," is commonly used to mean "to eat voraciously." It is interesting to note that as a noun, *trago* means "a drink." However, when used as a verb, tragar takes on the meaning of "to eat" • *¿Quieres echar un trago?*; Would you care for a drink? • *¿Qué quieres tragar?*; What would you like to eat?

SYNONYM -1: echarse un fogonazo *exp.* (Mexico) • (lit.): to throw oneself a flash.

SYNONYM -2: empinar el cacho *exp.* (Chile) • (lit.): to raise the piece.

SYNONYM -3: empinar el codo *exp.* • (lit.): to raise the elbow.

SYNONYM -4: pegarse un palo *exp.* (Cuba, Puerto Rico, Dominican Republic, Colombia) • (lit.): to stick oneself a gulp.

el brazo derecho *exp.* right-hand man • (lit.): the right arm.
example: Alfonso es **el brazo derecho** de Carlos.
translation: Alfonso is Carlos's **right-hand man**.

el hábito no hace al monje *exp.* you can't judge a book by its cover • (lit.): the habit (attire) doesn't make the monk.
example: Ramón siempre va muy bien vestido pero en realidad, no tiene dinero. ¡**El hábito no hace al monje**!
translation: Ramón is always dressed in expensive clothes but he actually has no money. **You can't judge a book by its cover**!

empezar con buen pie *exp.* to get off to a good start • (lit.): to begin with a good foot.
example: Esta mañana gané la lotería. **Empecé con buen pie**.
translation: I won the lottery this morning. **I got off to a good start**.

en brasas (estar) *exp.* to be on pins and needles, to be on tenterhooks, be uneasy. • (lit.): to be in live coal.
example: Susan está esperando ver si le dieron su ascenso. ¡**Está en brasas**!
translation: Susan is waiting to see if she got a promotion. She's **is on pins and needles**!

SYNONYM: estar como en brasas *exp.* • (lit.): to be like in live coal.

en cueros (estar) *exp.* naked, in one's birthday suit • (lit.): in one's own hide.
example: Ese bebé debe tener mucho frío porque **está en cueros**.
translation: That baby must be very cold because he is **completely naked**.

SYNONYM -1: en cueros vivos *exp.* • (lit.): in one's own living hide.

SYNONYM -2: en pelotas *exp.* (Spain) • (lit.): in balls.

SYNONYM -3: en el traje de Adán *exp.* • (lit.): in the suit of Adam.

SYNONYM -4: encuerado/a *adj.* • (lit.): skinned.

SYNONYM -5: en pila *f.* (Ecuador, Peru, Bolivia) • (lit.): heap, pile.

en el acto *exp.* • **1.** right away, immediately • **2.** in the act [of doing something] • (lit.): in the act.
example: Voy a hacer la tarea **en el acto**.
translation: I'm going to do my homework **right away**.

SYNONYM -1: acto continuo/seguido *exp.* same as definition **1** above • (lit.): continuous/consecutive act.

SYNONYM -2: ahora mismo *exp.* same as **1** and **2** above • (lit.): now the same.

SYNONYM -3: **de inmediato** *exp.* same as definition **1** above • (lit.): of immediate.

en el fondo *exp.* deep down, at heart • (lit.): at the bottom.
example: **En el fondo**, Felipe es una buena persona.
translation: **Deep down**, Felipe is a good person.

en el pellejo de alguien (estar) *exp.* to be in someone's shoes • (lit.): to be in someone's skin (hide).
example: No me gustaría **estar en su pellejo** cuando le pida un aumento al jefe.
translation: I wouldn't like **to be in his shoes** when he asks the boss for a raise.
SYNONYM: **en la piel de (estar)** *exp.* • (lit.): to be in one's skin.

en menos que canta un gallo *exp.* in a flash, as quick as a wink, in the winking of an eye • (lit.): in less time than a rooster can sing.
example: David siempre termina su almuerzo **en menos que canta un gallo**.
translation: David always finishes his lunch **in a flash**.

entrar por un oído y salir por el otro *exp.* to go in one ear and out the other • (lit.): to go in one ear and out the other.
example: Todo lo que le digo a Isabel **le entra por un oído y le sale por el otro**.
translation: Anything that I tell Isabel **goes in one ear and out the other**.
SYNONYM: **hacer caso omiso de** *exp.* • (lit.): to take no notice of.

escaso/a de fondos (estar/andar) *exp.* to be short of money • (lit.): to lack funds.
example: No puedo ir contigo al cine porque **estoy escaso de fondos**.
translation: I can't go with you to the movies because I'm **short of money**.
SYNONYM -1: **no tener ni un duro** *exp.* (Spain) • (lit.): no to have even a duro.

NOTE: **duro** *m.* a coin equal to five pesetas which is the national currency of Spain.

SYNONYM -2: **no tener plata** *exp.* (South America) • (lit.): not to have any silver.
ANTONYM -1: **estar podrido/a en dinero** *exp.* to be fithy-rich • (lit.): to be rotten in money.
ANTONYM -2: **tener más lana que un borrego** *exp.* to have more wool than a lamb.

estar de buenas *exp.* to be in a good mood • (lit.): to be in good.
example: Lynda es una mujer muy feliz. Siempre **está de buenas**.
translation: Lynda is a very happy woman. She is always **in a good mood**.
ANTONYM -1: **estar de malas** *exp.* to be in a bad mood • (lit.): to be in bad.
ANTONYM -2: **estar de un humor de perros** *exp.* • (lit.): to be in the mood of dogs.
ANTONYM -3: **tener malas pulgas** *exp.* • (lit.): to have bad fleas.

estar hecho una sopa *exp.* to be drenched, soaking wet • (lit.): to be made into a soup.
example: Susana llegó al trabajo **hecha una sopa**.

translation: Susana was **soaking wet** by the time she got to work.

SYNONYM: **estar empapado/a** *adj.* • (lit.): to be soaking wet.

faltar un tornillo *exp.* to have a screw lose • (lit.): to miss a screw.

example: Yo creo que a Paco le **falta un tornillo**.

translation: I think Paco **has a screw lose**.

SYNONYM -1: **estar chiflado/a** *exp.* • (lit.): to be crazy.

SYNONYM -2: **estar como una cabra** *exp.* • (lit.): to be like a goat.

SYNONYM -3: **estar tocado/a de la cabeza** *exp. (Spain)* • (lit.): to be touched in the head.

SYNONYM -4: **estar un poco loco/a** *exp.* • (lit.): to be a little bit crazy.

SYNONYM -5: **estar un poco sacado/a de onda** *exp. (Mexico)* • (lit.): to be a little taken from a wave.

SYNONYM -6: **tener flojos los tornillos** *exp.* • (lit.): to have loose screws.

SYNONYM -7: **tener los alambres pelados** *exp. (Chile)* • (lit.): to have peeled cables.

SYNONYM -8: **tener los cables cruzados** *exp. (Mexico)* • (lit.): to have crossed cables.

gastar saliva en balde *exp.* to waste one's breath [while explaining something to someone] • (lit.): to waste one's saliva in vain.

example: No me gusta **gastar saliva en balde**. Yo sé que de todas maneras no me entenderías.

translation: I don't like to **waste my breath**. I know you wouldn't understand me anyway.

gritar como unos descosidos *exp.* to scream one's lungs out, to scream out of control • (lit.): to scream like something unstiched.

example: Cuando fuimos al restaurante, mis niños estaban **gritando como unos descosidos**.

translation: When we went to the restaurant, my kids were **screaming out of control**.

NOTE: This expression comes from the verb *descoser* meaning "to unstitch." Therefore, this expression could be loosely translated as "to come apart at the seams."

haber gato encerrado *exp.* there's more than meets the eye, there's something fishy • (lit.): there's a locked cat (here).

example: Aquí **hay gato encerrado**. Esto no puede ser tan fácil.

translation: **There's more here than meets the eye**. This can't be so easy.

hablar [hasta] por los codos *exp.* to speak nonstop • (lit.): to talk even with the elbows.

example: Pablo siempre **habla hasta por los codos** cuando viene a mi casa.

translation: Pablo always **talks nonstop** when he comes to my house.

SYNONYM -1: hablar como loco/a *exp.* • (lit.): to speak like a crazy person.

SYNONYM -2: hablar como una cotorra *exp.* • (lit.): to talk like a parrot.

SYNONYM -3: no parar la boca *exp. (Mexico)*. • (lit.): not to let the mouth stop.

SYNONYM -4: ser de lengua larga *exp.* • (lit.): to be of long tongue.

hablar a mil por hora *exp.* to talk very fast, to talk a mile a minute • (lit.): to talk at one thousand kilometers per hour.

example: Lynda siempre **habla a mil por hora**.

translation: Lynda always **talks too fast**.

SYNONYM: hablar a borbotones *exp.* • (lit.): to talk like a torrent.

hablar como loco/a *exp.* to talk too much, to go on and on • (lit.): to talk like a crazy person.

example: Gabriela **habla como loca**. Nunca se calla.

translation: Gabriela **goes on and on**. She never shuts up.

SYNONYM -1: hablar como un loro *exp. (Spain)* • (lit.): to talk like a parrot.

SYNONYM -2: hablar como una cotorra *exp.* • (lit.): to talk like a parrot.

SYNONYM -3: hablar hasta por las narices *exp. (Spain)* • (lit.): to talk even through the nose.

SYNONYM -4: hablar más que siete *exp.* • (lit.): to talk more than seven (people).

SYNONYM -5: hablar por los codos *exp.* • (lit.): to talk through the elbows.

SYNONYM -6: no parar la boca *exp. (Mexico)* • (lit.): not to let the mouth stop.

hacer añicos *exp.* • **1.** (of objects) to smash to smithereens • **2.** (of paper) to rip to shreds • (lit.): to make (into) fragments or bits.

example: Elena **hizo añicos** mi plato favorito.

translation: Elena **smashed** my favorite plate **to smithereens**.

SYNONYM: hacer pedazitos *exp.* • (lit.): to make little pieces.

hacer acto de presencia *exp.* to put in an appearance, to show up • (lit.): to make an act of presence.

example: Jose Luis **hizo acto de presencia** en la fiesta de la escuela.

translation: Jose Luis **put in an appearance** at the school's party.

SYNONYM: presentarse *v.* • (lit.): to present oneself.

hacer el equipaje *exp.* to pack one's bags • (lit.): to make one's luggage.

example: Estoy **haciendo el equipaje** para ir a España.

translation: I'm **packing my bags** to go to Spain.

SYNONYM -1: empacar los belices *exp.* (Mexico) • (lit.): to pack the bags.

SYNONYM -2: hacer las maletas *exp.* • (lit.): to make one's trunks.

hacer frente a *exp.* to face up • (lit.): to make the front to.

example: Tenemos que **hacer frente** al hecho de que nuestra empresa está perdiendo dinero.

translation: We have **to face up to** the fact that our company is losing money.

hacer frente al hecho *exp*. to face up to the fact that • (lit.): to face up to the fact.

example: Tengo que **hacerle frente al hecho** de que tengo que trabajar tarde esta noche.

translation: I have **to face up to the fact that** I have to work late tonight.

SYNONYM: dar la cara a *exp*. • (lit.): to give the face to.

hacer las paces *exp*. to make up after a quarrel • (lit.): to make peace.

example: Josefina y Gerardo se pelearon pero luego **hicieron las paces**.

translation: Joesphina and Geraldo had a big fight but they finally **made up**.

SYNONYM: echar pelillos a la mar *exp*. (Southern Spain) to throw little hairs to the sea.

ANTONYM: romper con *exp*. to have a falling out • (lit.): to break with.

hacer mal/buen papel *exp*. to make a bad/good impression • (lit.): to do a bad/good (theatrical) role.

example: **Hiciste un buen papel** anoche.

translation: **You made a good impression** last night.

SYNONYM: caer mal/bien *exp*. • (lit.): to fall badly/well.

hacer puente *exp*. to take a long weekend, to take a three-day weekend • (lit.): to make a bridge.

example: La próxima semana voy a **hacer puente** y voy a ir a esquiar.

translation: Next week I'm going to take **a long weekend** and go skiing.

hacer su agosto *exp*. to make a killing • (lit.): to make one's August.

example: Alfredo y Eva **hicieron su agosto** en el casino.

translation: Alfredo y Eva **made a killing** at the casino.

hacer un gran furor *exp*. to be a big event, to make a big splash • (lit.): to make fury.

example: ¡Oí que **hiciste un gran furor** con el jefe!

translation: I heard you **made a big splash** with the boss!

SYNONYM: tener un éxito padre *exp*. (Mexico) to have a father success.

hacer[se] amigo de *exp*. to make friends with • (lit.): to make friends of.

example: **Me hice amigo de** Pedro porque es muy simpático.

translation: **I made friends with** Pedro because he's very nice.

SYNONYM: hacer buenas migas con *exp*. • (lit.): to make good bread crumbs with.

hacerse agua la boca *exp*. to make one's mouth water • (lit.): to make one's mouth water.

example: El olor de ese pan me está **haciendo agua la boca**.

translation: The smell of that bread is **making my mouth water**.

VARIATION: hacerse la boca agua *exp*.

harina de otro costal (ser) *exp*. to be another story, to be a horse of a different color • (lit.): to be flour of a different sack.

example: ¡Eso es **harina de otro costal**!

translation: That's **a different story**!

SYNONYM -1: no tener que ver con nada *exp*. • (lit.): not to have anything to do with anything.

SYNONYM -2: **no venir al cuento** *exp.* • (lit.): not to come to the story.

SYNONYM -3: **ser otro cantar** *exp.* • (lit.): to be another song.

hasta la coronilla de (estar) *exp.* to be fed up with, to be sick of [something or someone] • (lit.): to be up to the crown with.

example: Estoy **hasta la coronilla de** Marcos.

translation: I'm **fed up with** Marcos.

SYNONYM -1: **estar harto de [alguien]** *exp.* • (lit.): to be fed up with [someone].

SYNONYM -2: **estar hasta las cejas de** *exp.* • (lit.): to be up to the eyebrows.

hasta la fecha *exp.* to date, up till now • (lit.): until that date.

example: **Hasta la fecha** nunca había comido un pescado tan delicioso.

translation: **Up till now**, I have never had such delicious fish.

SYNONYM -1: **hasta el día de hoy** *exp.* • (lit.): until today.

SYNONYM -2: **hasta hoy** *exp.* • (lit.): until today.

SYNONYM -3: **hasta la actualidad** *exp.* • (lit.): until today.

hoy por hoy *exp.* as of right now • (lit.): today by today.

example: **Hoy por hoy** no tengo dinero.

translation: **As of right now**, I don't have money to pay you.

ir a medias *exp.* to go halfsies, fifty-fifty • (lit.): to go halves.

example: Cuando salimos a cenar siempre **vamos a medias**.

translation: When we go out for dinner we always split everything **fifty-fifty** on the bill.

SYNONYM -1: **ir a la mitad** *exp.* • (lit.): to go to the half.

SYNONYM -2: **ir mitad mitad** *exp.* • (lit.): to go half-half.

ir al asunto *exp.* to get down to the facts • (lit.): to go to the subject.

example: ¡**Vamos al asunto**!

translation: **Let's get down to the facts**!

ir sin decir *exp.* to go without saying • (lit.): to go without saying.

example: Eso **va sin decir**.

translation: That **goes without saying**.

jugar el todo por el todo *exp.* to risk everything, to go for it • (lit.): to play (risk) everything for everything.

example: Cuando invertí en la bolsa, me **jugé el todo por el todo**.

translation: When I invested in the stock market, I **risked everything**.

la gota que derrama el vaso (ser) *exp.* to be the last straw, the straw that broke the camel's back • (lit.): to be the drop that makes the glass spill over.

example: Elle me mintió anoche. ¡Eso ya **fue la gota que derramó el vaso**!

translation: She lied to me last night. That's **the last straw**!

SYNONYM -1: **es el colmo** *exp.* • (lit.): it is the height (or: that's the limit).

SYNONYM -2: **la última gota que hace rebosar la copa** *exp.* • (lit.): the last drop that makes the glass overflow.

SYNONYM -3: **¡No faltaba más! / ¡Lo que faltaba! / ¡Sólo faltaba eso!** *exp.* • (lit.): Nothing else was missing! / What was missing! / Only that was missing!

SYNONYM -4: **la gota que colmó el vaso (ser)** *exp.* • (lit.): to be the drop that makes the glass spill over.

las malas lenguas *exp.* gossip • (lit.): the bad tongues.

example: Dicen **las malas lenguas** que Darío va a dejar a Lucía por otra mujer.

translation: According to **gossip**, Dario is going to leave Lucia for another woman.

llamar al pan pan y al vino vino *exp.* to call it like it is • (lit.): to call bread, bread and wine, wine.

example: Yo siempre **llamo al pan pan y al vino vino**.

translation: I always **call it like it is**.

SYNONYM: **llamar a las cosas por su nombre** *exp.* • (lit.): to call things by their name.

llamar la atención *exp.* to attract attention • (lit.): to call for attention.

example: Magda siempre **llama la atención** cuando se pone esa minifalda.

translation: Magda always **attracts attention** when she wears that mini-skirt.

llevar los pantalones *exp.* to wear the pants, to be in command • (lit.): to wear the pants.

example: En mi casa yo **llevo los pantalones**.

translation: In my house, **I wear the pants in the family**.

SYNONYM -1: **llevar los calzones** *exp.* • (lit.): to wear underwear.

SYNONYM -2: **llevar la batuta** *exp.* • (lit.): to carry the baton.

llevar/seguir la corriente *exp.* to humor someone, to go along with • (lit.): to carry/follow the current to someone.

example: Me gusta **llevarle la corriente** a mi esposa porque no me gusta discutir con ella.

translation: I like **to humor** my wife because I don't like to argue with her.

NOTE: This comes from the verb *correr* meaning "to run." Therefore, una corriente could be loosely translated as "a woman who runs around with more than one man."

llevarse como perro y gato *exp.* not to get along, to fight like cats and dogs • (lit.): to carry each other like dog and cat.

example: Teresa y Carlos **se llevan como perro y gato**.

translation: Teresa and Carlos **fight like cats and dogs**.

NOTE: Make sure to be aware of the difference between the Spanish expression and its English equivalent. In the Spanish expression, it's *perro y gato*; "dog and cat," both singular. However, in English the order is opposite; "cats and dogs," both plural.

SYNONYM -1: **llevarse mal con** *exp.* • (lit.): to carry oneself off badly with.

SYNONYM -2: **no hacer buenas migas con** *exp.* • (lit.): not to make good bread crumbs with.

ANTONYM -1: **llevarse bien con** *exp.* to get along well with • (lit.): to carry oneself off well with.

ANTONYM -2: **hacer buenas migas con** *exp.* to get along well with • (lit.): to make good bread crumbs with.

llover a cántaros *exp.* to rain cats and dogs • (lit.): to rain pitcherfuls.
example: No podemos ir al parque porque está **lloviendo a cántaros**.
translation: We can't go to the park because **it's raining cats and dogs**.

SYNONYM -1: **caer burros aparejados** *exp.* (Cuba, Puerto Rico, Dominican Republic) • (lit.): to fall prepared donkeys.

SYNONYM -2: **caer el diluvio** *exp.* • (lit.): to fall the Flood (as in the Bible).

SYNONYM -3: **caer un chaparrón** *exp.* • (lit.): to fall a downpour.

SYNONYM -4: **llover a chorros** *exp.* • (lit.): to rain in spurts.

SYNONYM -5: **llover con rabia** *exp.* (Cuba, Puerto Rico, Dominican Republic, Southern Spain) • (lit.): to rain with anger (or fury).

lo dicho, dicho *exp.* what I said, goes • (lit.): I said it, said.
example: ¡Ya no te quiero ver más! **Lo dicho, dicho.**

translation: I don't want to see you again! **What I said, goes.**

loco/a de remate (estar) *exp.* to be totally crazy, nuts, hopelessly mad • (lit.): crazy of end.
example: Eduardo está **loco de remate**. Siempre habla consigo mismo en público.
translation: Eduardo is **totally crazy**. He always talks to himself in public.

SYNONYM -1: **como una cabra (estar)** *exp.* • (lit.): to be like a goat.

SYNONYM -2: **loco/a de atar (estar)** *exp.* • (lit.): to be crazy to restrict.

más vale prevenir que curar *exp.* better to be safe than sorry • (lit.): it's worth more to prevent than to cure.
example: **Más vale prevenir que curar**. Voy a traer el paraguas por si llueve.
translation: **Better safe than sorry**. I'm going to bring my umbrella just in case it rains.

más vale tarde que nunca *exp.* better late than never • (lit.): it is worth more late than never.
example: Menos mal que llegaste. **Más vale tarde que nunca**.
translation: Good thing you showed up. **Better late than never**.

mandar a alguien a bañar *exp.* to tell someone to go take a flying leap, to tell someone to go fly a kite • (lit.): to send someone to take a bath.
example (1): **¡Vete a bañar!**

translation: **Go fly a kite**!

example (2): Cuando Adolfo me pidió dinero por tercera vez, ¡**lo mandé a bañar**!

translation: When Adolfo asked me to lend him money for the third time, I told him **to go take a flying leap**!

SYNONYM -1: ¡**Vete a echar pulgas a otra parte!** *exp.* • (lit.): Go throw fleas somewhere else.

SYNONYM -2: ¡**Vete a freír chongos!** *exp.* (Mexico) • (lit.): Go fry buns!

SYNONYM -3: ¡**Vete a freír esparragos!** *exp.* • (lit.): Go fry asparagus.

SYNONYM -4: ¡**Vete a freír mocos!** *exp.* (Ecuador, Peru, Bolivia) • (lit.): Go fry mucus!

SYNONYM -5: ¡**Vete a freír monos!** *exp.* (Colombia & Spain) • (lit.): Go fry monkeys!

SYNONYM -6: ¡**Vete a ver si ya puso la cochina/puerca!** *exp.* (Latin America) • (lit.): Go see if the sow has already laid an egg.

meter las narices en lo que a uno no le importa *exp.* to butt into other people's business, to stick one's nose into everything • (lit.): to put the nose into that which doesn't concern one.

example: Darío siempre **mete las narices donde no le importa**.

translation: Dario always **sticks his nose into everything**.

meterse en un [buen] berenjenal *exp.* to get oneself into a [real] jam, to get oneself into a fine mess • (lit.): to get into a good eggplant patch.

example: No mientas sobre lo que pasó o te vas a **meter en un buen berenjenal**.

translation: Everytime I go to that bar **I get myself into a mess**.

SYNONYM: **meterse en un buen lío** *exp.* • (lit.): to put oneself in a good bundle.

mirar por sus [proprios] intereses *exp.* to look out for oneself, to look out for number one • (lit.): to look out for one's [own] interests.

example: A Simón no le importa la gente. Solo **mira por sus [propios] intereses**.

translation: Simón doesn't care about other people. He only **looks out for number one**.

SYNONYM: **preocuparse solo de uno mismo** *exp.* to worry only about oneself • (lit.): [same].

misma imagen (ser la) *exp.* to be the spitting image of • (lit.): to be the same image.

example: David es **la misma imagen** que su padre.

translation: David is the **spitting image** of his father.

SYNONYM -1: **ser escupido/a de** *exp.* • (lit.): to be the spit of.

SYNONYM -2: **ser viva imagen de** *exp.* • (lit.): to be the live image of.

morderse la lengua *exp.* to hold or control one's tongue • (lit.): to bite one's tongue.

example: ¡**Muérdete la lengua**!

translation: **Bite your tongue**!

ANTONYM -1: **cantar claro** *exp.* to speak clearly • (lit.): to sing clearly.

ANTONYM -2: **no morderse la lengua** *exp.* not to mince words, to speak straight from the shoulder • (lit.): not to bite one's tongue.

ANTONYM -3: **ser claridoso/a** *exp.* (Venezuela, central America) • (lit.): to be very clear.

morir de ganas *exp.* to be dying to do something, to feel like • (lit.): to die of wish.

example: **Me muero de ganas** por ver a María.

translation: **I'm dying** to see Maria.

SYNONYM: **tener muchas ganas de** *exp.* • (lit.): to have many desires to.

mucho ruido y pocas nueces *exp.* much ado about nothing, a big fuss about nothing • (lit.): a lot of noise and very few walnuts.

example: Antonio tuvo una emergencia y me pidió que viniera enseguida. Pero en realidad era **mucho ruido y pocas nueces**.

translation: Antonio had an emergency and asked me to come over immediately. But it was really **a big fuss about nothing**.

muy ligero/a de palabra (ser) *exp.* to be a blabbermouth • (lit.): to be very light in words.

example: Rafael es **muy ligero de palabra**. Le gusta hablar demasiado.

translation: Rafael is a **blabbermouth**. He likes to talk too much.

SYNONYM -1: **charlatán (ser un)** *adj.* • (lit.): to be a charlatan.

SYNONYM -2: **chismoso (ser un)** *adj.* • (lit.): to be a gossip.

SYNONYM -3: **cuentista (ser un)** *adj.* • (lit.): to be a story teller.

nacer de pie *exp.* to be born lucky • (lit.): to be born (on foot) standing.

example: Yo he **nacido de pie**.

translation: I was **born lucky**.

SYNONYM -1: **nacer con estrella** *exp.* • (lit.): to be born with star.

SYNONYM -2: **nacer parado/a** *exp.* • (lit.): to be born standing.

ANTONYM -1: **nacer al revés** *exp.* to be born unlucky • (lit.): to be born backwards.

ANTONYM -2: **nacer estrellado/a** *exp.* to be born unlucky • (lit.): to be born crashed.

nadar entre dos aguas *exp.* to be undecided, to be on the fence, not to be able to make up one's mind • (lit.): to swim between two waters.

example: Roberto no sabe qué coche comprar. Está **nadando entre dos aguas**.

translation: Roberto doesn't know what car to buy. He **can't make up his mind**.

SYNONYM -1: **entre azul y buenas noches** *exp.* • (lit.): between blue and a good night.

SYNONYM -2: **ni fu ni fa** *exp.* (Spain) • (lit.): not "fu" nor "fa."

SYNONYM -3: **ni un sí ni un no** *exp.* • (lit.): not a yes nor a no.

nervios de punta (tener los) *exp.* to be edgy, to be very nervous • (lit.): to have one's nerves on end.

example: **¡Tengo los nervios de punta!**

translation: **I'm so edgy!**

SYNONYM: **estar hecho un manojo de nervios** *exp.* to be a bundle of nerves • (lit.): to be made a bundle of nerves.

ni mucho menos *exp.* far from it • (lit.): not even much less.

example: ¿Lo pasaste bien en la fiesta? **Ni mucho menos**.

translation: Did you have a good time at the party? **Far from it**.

SYNONYM: ¡Qué va! *exp.* (Spain)• (lit.): What goes!

no caber de contento *exp.* to be very happy, to be excited [about something] • (lit.): not to fit because one is so happy.

example: Alfredo **no cabe de contento** porque tiene una novia nueva.

translation: Alfredo **couldn't be happier** because he has a new girlfriend.

no dar el brazo a torcer *exp.* to stick to one's guns, not to give in, not to have one's arm twisted • (lit.): not to give one's arm to be twisted.

example: Pablo **nunca da su brazo a torcer**. Es muy testarudo.

translation: Pablo always **sticks to his guns**. He's very stubborn.

ANTONYM: dar el brazo a torcer *exp.* to give in, to have one's arm twisted • (lit.): to give one's arm to be twisted.

no entender ni papa *exp.* not to understand a thing • (lit.): not to understand a potato.

example: Cuando voy a clase de matemáticas, **no entiendo ni papa**.

translation: When I go to my math class, **I don't understand a thing**.

no hay ni cuatro gatos *exp.* there's hardly a soul • (lit.): not to be even four cats.

example: En esta fiesta **no hay ni cuatro gatos**.

translation: There's **hardly a soul** at this party.

ANTONYM -1: estar de bote en bote *exp.* to be very crowded • (lit.): to be from boat to boat.

ANTONYM -2: estar hasta los botes *exp.* to be very crowed • (lit.): to be up to the boats.

no importar un bledo *exp.* not to give a darn about (something) • (lit.): it doesn't matter one goosefoot plant.

example: Irene no me invitó a su fiesta. Pero a mí **no me importa un bledo**. A mí mo me gusta ella de todas maneras.

translation: Irena didn't invite me to her party. But I **don't give a darn**. I don't like her anyway.

SYNONYM: no importar un huevo *exp.* • (lit.): it doesn't matter one egg.

NOTE: This expression is somewhat rude and should be used with caution since *huevo* (literally meaning "egg") means "testicle" in many Spanish-speaking countries.

no inventar la pólvora *exp.* not to be very bright • (lit.): not to invent gunpowder.

example: Mauricio **no ha inventado la pólvora**.

translation: Mauricio **is not very bright**.

SYNONYM -1: no estar muy despierto *exp.* • (lit.): not to be very awake.

SYNONYM -2: no ser muy vivo *exp.* (Mexico) • (lit.): not to be very alive.

no mover un dedo *exp.* not to lift a finger • (lit.): not to move a finger.

example: Andrés **nunca mueve un dedo**.

translation: Andrés **never lifts a finger**.

SYNONYM: no levantar un dedo *exp.* • (lit.): not to lift a finger.

no poder más *exp.* to be exhausted • (lit.): to be unable to do anything more.

example: ¡**No puedo más**! Me voy a dormir.

translation: **I'm exhausted**! I'm going to sleep.

SYNONYM -1: estar más muerto/a que vivo/a *exp.* • (lit.): to be more dead than alive.

SYNONYM -2: estar molido/a *adj.* to be ground up or pulverized.

SYNONYM -3: estar muerto/a *adj.* to be dead (tired).

SYNONYM -4: tener los huesos molidos *exp.* • (lit.): to have one's bones ground up (or more literally: to be tired to the bone).

no poder ver a alguien ni en pintura *exp.* not to be able to stand someone • (lit.): not to be able to look at a painting of someone (as the mere image would be too much to bear).

example: No puedo **ver a Gonzalo ni en pintura**.

translation: I **can't stand the site of Gonzalo**.

SYNONYM -1: no poder con *exp.* • (lit.): not to be able to handle [something/someone].

SYNONYM -2: no tragar a alguien *exp.* • (lit.): not to swallow someone.

no querer tener nada que ver con alguien *exp.* not want to have anything to do with someone • (lit.): not to want to have anything to see with someone.

example: **No quiero tener nada que ver con** Rigoberto porque está loco.

translation: **I don't want to have anything to do with Rigoberto** because he's crazy.

SYNONYM: no querer liarse con alguien *exp.* • (lit.): not to want to get involved with someone.

no ser cosa de juego *exp.* to be no laughing matter • (lit.): not to be a thing of game.

example: ¡Esto **no es cosa de juego**!

translation: This **is no laughing matter**!

no tener ni pies ni cabeza *exp.* not to make any sense • (lit.): not to have feet or head.

example: Lo que estás diciendo **no tiene ni pies ni cabeza**.

translation: What you're saying **doesn't make any sense**.

no tener ni un pelo de tonto/a *exp.* to be nobody's fool • (lit.): not to have even one hair of stupid.

example: Pedro **no tiene ni un pelo de tonto**.

translation: Pedro is **nobody's fool**.

SYNONYM: ser muy vivo/a *exp.* (Mexico) • (lit.): to be very alive.

no tener pelos en la lengua *exp.* not to mince words, to be outspoken, not to hold back any punches • (lit.): not to have hairs on the tongue.

example: Rafael es una persona muy honesta. **No tiene pelos en la lengua**.

translation: Rafael is a very honest person. **He doesn't hold back any punches**.

pagar al contado *exp.* to pay cash
• (lit.): to pay counted.
<u>example:</u> Mauricio debe tener mucho dinero porque siempre **paga todo al contado**.
<u>translation:</u> Mauricio must have a lot of money because he always **pays everything in cash**.

SYNONYM -1: **pagar a tocateja** *exp.* • (lit.): to pay tocateja style (no translation for tocateja).

SYNONYM -2: **pagar con billete** *exp.* (Mexico) • (lit.): to pay with notes.

SYNONYM -3: **pagar con dinero contante y sonante** *exp.* • (lit.): to pay with money that you can actually count and hear.

pagar la casa *exp.* to pay rent • (lit.): to pay the house.
<u>example:</u> No tengo dinero porque ayer **pagué la casa**.
<u>translation:</u> I don't have any money because yesterday I **paid my rent**.

pan comido (ser) *exp.* to be easy, a cinch • (lit.): to be eaten bread.
<u>example:</u> Este examen es **pan comido**.
<u>translation:</u> This test is **a cinch**.
SYNONYM: **estar tirado/a** *adj.* (Spain) • (lit.): to be thrown away • Este examen está tirado; This test is so easy.

para chuparse los dedos *exp.* said of something delicious • (lit.): to suck or lick one's fingers.
<u>example:</u> Esta comida está **para chuparse los dedos**.
<u>translation:</u> This food is **delicious**.

NOTE: A popular Spanish advertisement goes as follows: *Kentucky Fried Chicken está para chuparse los dedos;* Kentucky Fried Chicken is finger lickin' good.

SYNONYM: **estar a toda madre** *exp.* (Mexico) • This popular Mexican expression is used to express enthusiasm about food as well as situations • (lit.): to be like an entire mother.

partirle el corazón a alguien *exp.* to break someone's heart • (lit.): to break someone's heart.
<u>example:</u> Parece que Laura **le rompió el corazón a Felipe**.
<u>translation:</u> It looks like Laura **broke Felipe's heart**.

pasar por alto *exp.* to overlook • (lit.): to overpass.
<u>example:</u> Yo iba a **pasar por alto** algunas cosas, pero esto es demasiado.
<u>translation:</u> I was going **to overlook** some things, but this is too much.

pasarse de la raya *exp.* to go too far, to overstep one's bounds • (lit.): to cross the line.
<u>example:</u> Yo creo que Jaime **se pasó de la raya** cuando intentó besar a Isabel.
<u>translation:</u> I think Jaime **went a little too far** when he tried to kiss Isabel.
NOTE: This expression is so popular among Spanish-speakers, that often *de la raya* is omitted since it is already understood by the listener. For example: Te has pasado; You went too far.

pegarse como una ladilla *exp.* to stick to someone like glue • (lit.): to stick to someone like a crab (as in pubic lice).

example: Alberto es un pesado. Siempre **se pega como una ladilla**.

translation: Alberto is a pain. He **sticks to me like glue**.

NOTE: This expression is considered somewhat crude and should be used with discretion.

pensar para sus adentros *exp.* to think to oneself • (lit.): to think by one's insides.

example: Estaba yo **pensando para mis adentros** que sería bueno hacer un viaje a Paris este verano.

translation: I was **thinking to myself** that it would be nice to go on a trip to Paris next summer.

perder el habla *exp.* to be speechless • (lit.): to lose one's speech.

example: **Perdí el habla** cuando vi a María en ese vestido. ¡Era tan corto!

translation: **I was speechless** when I saw Maria wearing that dress. It was so short!

SYNONYM: **quedarse mudo/a** *exp.* • (lit.): to remain/become mute.

perder los estribos *exp.* to lose control, to lose one's head, to lose one's temper • (lit.): to lose the stirrups.

example: Como sigas portándote así, voy a **perder los estribos**.

translation: If you continue to behave this way, I'm going to **lose my temper**.

SYNONYM -1: **perder la calma** *exp.* • (lit.): to lose one's calm.

SYNONYM -2: **perder la paciencia** *exp.* • to lose one's patience.

poco a poco *exp.* little by little • (lit.): little to little.

example: **Poco a poco** terminé todo el proyecto.

translation: **Little by little** I finished the whole project.

poderoso caballero es Don Dinero *exp.* money makes the world go 'round, money talks • (lit.): Mr. money is a powerful gentleman.

example: Me dieron la mejor mesa del restaurante. **Poderoso caballero es Don Dinero**.

translation: They gave me the best table in the restaurant. **Money makes the world go 'round**.

poner a alguien como un trapo *exp.* to rake someone over the coals, to read someone the riot act • (lit.): to put someone like a rag.

example: Juan **puso al mesero como un trapo** porque no le trajo la comida a tiempo.

translation: Juan **raked the waiter over the coals** because he didn't bring him his meal on time.

poner al corriente *exp.* to bring up-to-date, to inform, to give the lowdown • (lit.): to put in the current or in the flow of knowledge.

example: Te voy a **poner al corriente** de lo que sucedió ayer en la oficina.

translation: I'm going to **bring you up-to-date** about what happened yesterday at the office.

SYNONYM: poner al día *exp.* • (lit.): to put to the day.

poner al día *exp.* to bring up-to-date, to inform, to give the lowdown • (lit.): to put to the day.

example: Pedro, ¡te voy a **poner al día**! Han pasado muchas cosas desde que te fuiste de vacaciones.

translation: Pedro, I'm going **to bring you up to date**! A lot of things happened while you were on vacation.

SYNONYM: poner al tanto *exp.* • (lit.): to put one at the point (in a score).

poner el grito al cielo *exp.* to raise the roof, to scream with rage, to hit the ceiling • (lit.): to put a scream to the sky.

example: Lynda **puso el grito al cielo** cuando vio que la casa estaba muy sucia.

translation: Lynda **hit the ceiling** when she found out that the house was a real mess.

VARIATION: **poner en el grito al cielo** *exp.* • (lit.): to make a scandal.

SYNONYM -1: **formar/armar un follón** *exp. (Spain).* • (lit.): to make a scandal.

SYNONYM -2: **hacer/formar un escándalo** *exp.* • (lit.): to make a scandal.

poner en ridículo *exp.* to make a fool out of someone • (lit.): to put [someone] in ridiculous.

example: Jorge está **poniendo en ridículo** a su jefe a propósito.

translation: Jorge is **making a fool out of** his boss on purpose.

poner las cartas sobre la mesa *exp.* to to put one's cards on the table • (lit.): to put the cards on the table.

example: Si vas a hablar conmigo, **pon las cartas sobre la mesa**.

translation: If you're going to talk to me, **put all your cards on the table**.

poner[se] colorado/a *exp.* to blush, to turn red • (lit.): to put oneself (to become) red.

example: Si sigues hablando así me voy a **poner rojo**.

translation: If you continue to talk like that, I'm going **to turn red**.

VARIATION: **poner[se] rojo/a** *exp.* • (lit.): to put oneself (to become) red.

SYNONYM: **acholar[se]** *v.* (Ecuador, Peru) • (lit.): to shame (oneself).

SYNONYM -2: **ruborizar[se]** *v.* (Latin America) • (lit.): to make oneself blush.

ponerse a flote *exp.* to get back up on one's own two feet again • (lit.): to put oneself afloat.

example: Después de comenzar su nuevo trabajo, Alberto **se puso a flote** otra vez.

translation: After starting his new job, Alberto is **back on his feet**.

SYNONYM: **levantar la cabeza** *exp.* • (lit.): to lift the head.

NOTE: This could be best compared to the American expression, "to hold up one's head" or "to pull oneself back up."

ponerse los pelos de punta *exp.* to have one's hair stand on end • (lit.): to put one's hairs on end.

example: **Se me pusieron los pelos de punta** cuando vi al elefante escaparse del zoológico.

translation: **My hair stood on end** when I saw the elephant escaping from the zoo.

por fortuna *exp.* fortunately • (lit.): by fortune.

example: Hoy hubo una gran explosión en la fábrica pero **por fortuna** no hubo heridos.

translation: There was a big explosion at the factory today but **fortunately** no one was hurt.

por las buenas o por las malas *exp.* whether one likes it or not, one way or another • (lit.): by the goods or by the bads.

example: David va a ganar la carrera **por las buenas o por las malas**.

translation: David is going to win the race **one way or another**.

VARIATION: **a las buenas o a las malas** *exp.* • (lit.): to the good ones or to the bad ones.

SYNONYM: **de una manera u otra** *exp.* • (lit.): one way or another.

por las nubes (estar) *exp.* astronomical, sky high • (lit.): to be by the clouds.

example: Los precios de esta tienda están **por las nubes**.

translation: Prices at this store are **astronomical**.

por lo general *exp.* as a general rule, usually • (lit.): generally.

example: **Por lo general** no me gusta comer mucha carne roja.

translation: **As a general rule**, I don't like to eat too much red meat.

SYNONYM -1: **por lo común** *exp.* • (lit.): by the common.

SYNONYM -2: **por lo regular** *exp.* • (lit.): by the regular.

por ningún motivo *exp.* under no circumstances • (lit.): by no reason.

example: **Por ningún motivo** me hables en ese tono de voz.

translation: **Under no circumstances** are you to talk to me using that tone of voice.

SYNONYM: **bajo ningún motivo** *exp.* • (lit.): under no reason.

por si acaso *exp.* just in case • (lit.): by if case.

example: Voy a llevar mi abrigo **por si acaso** hace frío más tarde.

translation: I'm going to bring my coat with me **just in case** it gets colder later.

probar fortuna *exp.* to try one's luck • (lit.): to try fortune.

example: Cuando voy a Las Vegas me gusta **probar fortuna** en el casino.

translation: When I go to Las Vegas I enjoy **trying my luck** in the casino.

quedarse mudo/a *exp.* to be speechless, not to be able to respond, to be flabbergasted • (lit.): to remain mute.

example: Antonio **se quedó mudo** cuando vio a Luisa en ese vestido anaranjado.

translation: Antonio **was flabbergasted** when he saw Luisa wearing that orange dress.

SYNONYM -1: **dejar sin habla** *exp.* • (lit.): to leave [someone] without speech.

SYNONYM -2: **perder el habla** *exp.* • (lit.): to lose the speech.

¿Qué mosca te ha picado? *exp.* What's bugging you? • (lit.): What fly has bitten you?

example: No se **qué mosca te ha picado** pero no me gusta cuando estás de mal humor.

translation: I don't know **what's eating you**, but I don't like it when you are in such a bad mood.

SYNONYM: **¿Qué bicho te ha picado?** *exp.* • (lit.): What bug has bitten you?

quitarse años *exp.* to lie about one's age • (lit.): to take off years.

example: Teresa siempre **se quita años**.

translation: Teresa always **lies about her age**.

rabo del ojo (mirar/ver por el) *exp.* to look/to see out of the corner of the eye • (lit.): to look/to see by the tail of the eye.

example: **Miré con el rabo del ojo** y vi que todo el mundo se estaba fijando en mí.

translation: **I looked out of the corner of my eye** and I saw that everybody was staring at me.

SYNONYM: mirar/ver de reojo *exp.* • (lit.): to look suspiciously at.

rascarse el bolsillo *exp.* to cough up money • (lit.): to scratch one's pocket.

example: Estoy cansado de **rascarme el bolsillo** para pagar la renta cada mes. A lo mejor es hora de que compre una casa.

translation: I'm tired of **coughing up money** every month on rent. Maybe it's time for me to buy a house.

romper el hielo *exp.* to break the ice • (lit.): to break the ice.

example: Hice una broma para **romper el hielo**.

translation: I told a joke **to break the ice**.

romper la crisma a alguien *exp.* to ring someone's neck. • (lit.): to break someone's chrism.

example: Como no te portes bien, **te voy a romper la crisma**.

translation: If you don't behave well, I'm **going to ring your neck**.

SYNONYM -1: romperle el alma a alguien *exp.* • (lit.): to break someone's soul.

SYNONYM -2: romperle el bautismo a alguien *exp.* • (lit.): to break one's baptism.

SYNONYM -3: romperle la cara a alguien *exp.* to smash someone's face • (lit.): [same].

SYNONYM -4: romperle la nariz [a alguien] *exp.* • (lit.): to break someone's nose.

saltar a la vista *exp.* to be obvious • (lit.): to jump to the sight.

example: **Salta a la vista** que Pepe hace ejercicio diariamente.

translation: **It's obvious** that Pepe exercises daily.

SYNONYM: saltar a los ojos *exp.* • (lit.): to jump to the eyes.

sin falta *exp.* without fail • (lit.): without fail.

example: Mañana voy a comprarme un abrigo nuevo **sin falta**.

translation: Tomorrow I'm going to buy myself a new coat **without fail**.

sin faltar una coma *exp.* down to the last detail • (lit.): without missing a comma.

example: Te voy a contar lo que pasó **sin faltar una coma**.

translation: I'm going to tell you what happened **down to the last detail**.

SYNONYM: con puntos y comas *exp.* • (lit.): with periods and commas.

sobre gustos no hay nada escrito *exp.* to each his own [taste] • (lit.): on tastes, there is nothing written (meaning: when it come to tastes, there are no rules).

example: ¡Mira qué zapatos lleva Adolfo! **Sobre gustos no hay nada escrito**.

translation: Look at the shoes Adolfo is wearing! **To each his own taste**.

SYNONYM: **en gustos se rompen géneros** *exp.* • (lit.): in tastes one can break genders.

subir a la cabeza *exp.* • to go to one's head (said of conceit or alcohol) • (lit.): to go up to one's head.

example: Parece que a Arturo se le **subió a la cabeza** el hecho de que ahora es supervisor.

translation: It seems that the fact that Arturo is now a supervisor **went to his head**.

sudar la gota gorda *exp.* to sweat blood, to make a superhuman effort • (lit.): to sweat the fat drop.

example: Cuando voy al gimnasio siempre **sudo la gota gorda**.

translation: When I go to the gym, I always **sweat bullets**.

SYNONYM: **sudar petróleo** *exp.* • (lit.): to sweat petroleum.

T

tan claro como el agua (estar) *exp.* it's as plain as the nose on one's face • (lit.): as clear as water.

example: ¡Está **tan claro como el agua**! Guillermo odia su trabajo.

translation: It's **as plain as day**! Guillermo hates his job.

SYNONYM: **tan claro como que yo me llamo [fill in your own name]** *exp.* • (lit.): it's as clear as my name is [fill in your own name].

tener algo en la punta de la lengua *exp.* to have something on the tip of the tongue • (lit.): [same].

example: No me acuerdo de cómo se llama ese tipo, pero lo **tengo en la punta de la lengua**.

translation: I don't remember that guy's name but **it's on the tip of my tongue**.

tener don de gentes *exp.* to have a way with people • (lit.): to have a gift of people.

example: Estefanía **tiene don de gentes**.

translation: Estefania **has a way with people**.

tener fama de *exp.* to have a reputation for • (lit.): to have fame for.

example: Ese restaurante **tiene fama de** servir buena comida.

translation: That restaurant **has a reputation for** good food.

tener los huesos molidos *exp.* to be wiped out, exhausted, ready to collapse • (lit.): to have ground up bones.

example: He trabajado todo el día. **Tengo los huesos molidos**.

translation: I've worked all day long. **I'm wiped out**.

SYNONYM -1: **estar hecho/a polvo** *exp.* (Spain) • (lit.): to be made of dust.

SYNONYM -2: **estar hecho/a un trapo** *exp.* to be made of rag.

SYNONYM -3: **estar reventado/a** *adj.* • (lit.): to be smashed.

tener madera para *exp.* to have what it takes, to be cut out for [something] • (lit.): to have the wood for [something].

example: Augusto no **tiene madera para** ser bombero.

translation: Augusto doesn't **have what it takes** to be a firefighter.

SYNONYM: **estar hecho/a para** *exp.* • (lit.): to be made for.

tener malas pulgas *exp.* to be irritable, ill-tempered • (lit.): to have bad fleas.

example: José siempre **tiene malas pulgas**.

translation: Jose is always so **irritable**.

SYNONYM -1: **tener mal humor** *exp.* • (lit.): to have bad humor or mood.

SYNONYM -2: **tener un humor de perros** *exp.* • (lit.): to have a mood of dogs.

tener pájaros en la cabeza *exp.* to be crazy, to have a screw lose • (lit.): to have birds in the head.

example: Daniel **tiene pájaros en la cabeza**.

translation: Daniel **has a screw lose**.

SYNONYM -1: **estar como una cabra** *exp.* • (lit.): to be like a goat.

SYNONYM -2: **estar loco/a de remate** *exp.* • (lit.): to be crazy in the end.

SYNONYM -3: **estar tocado/a** *exp.* (Spain) • (lit.): to be touched.

SYNONYM -4: **faltar un tornillo** *exp.* (lit.): to have a screw missing.

tiempo de perros *exp.* lousy weather • (lit.): weather of dogs.

example: Hoy hace un **tiempo de perros**.

translation: Today we're having **lousy weather**.

tirarse/jalarse de los pelos *exp.* to squabble, to have a fight (either verbally or physically) • (lit.): to pull from one's hairs.

example: Verónica y Luis se estaban **tirando de los pelos**.

translation: Veronica and Luis were **having a big fight**.

NOTE: The verb *jalarse* is used primarily in Mexico.

todo oídos (ser) *exp.* to be all ears • (lit.): to be all ears.

example: Dime lo que pasó. **Soy todo oídos**.

translation: Tell me what happened. **I'm all ears**.

tomar a broma *exp.* to take lightly • (lit.): to take like a joke.

example: ¡**No te lo tomes a broma**! Estoy hablado en serio.

translation: **Don't take it lightly**! I'm serious.

ANTONYM: **tomar en serio** *exp.* to take it seriously • (lit.): to take it seriously.

tomar el pelo a alguien *exp.* to pull someone's leg • (lit.): to take someone's hair.

example: Creo que me estás **tomando el pelo**.

translation: I think you're **pulling my leg**.

SYNONYM: **hacerle guaje a uno** *exp.* (Mexico) • (lit.): to make a fool of someone.

tomar un poco de aire fresco *exp.* to get some fresh air • (lit.): to take a little fresh air.

example: Me duele la cabeza. Voy a **tomar un poco de aire fresco**.

translation: I have a headache. I'm going **to get some fresh air**.

SYNONYM: **tomar el fresco** *exp.* • (lit.): to take some fresh (air).

tomarle la palabra a alguien
exp. to take someone at his/her word • (lit.): to take the word to someone.
example: Está bien. Voy a **tomarte la palabra**.
translation: O.K. I'm going **to take you at your word**.

torcer el brazo de alguien *exp.* to convince someone to do something, to twist someone's arm • (lit.): to twist one's arm.
example: Bueno, **me has torcido el brazo**. Mañana te ayudo a limpiar la casa.
translation: Well, **you twisted my arm**. Tomorrow I'll help you do some house cleaning.

traer por los pelos *exp.* to be farfetched • (lit.): to be carried by the hairs.
example: Me parece que su cuento es **traído por los pelos**.
translation: I think his story is a little **farfetched**.

tragar el anzuelo *exp.* to swallow it hook, line, and sinker • (lit.): to swallow the hook.
example: Alberto **se tragó el anzuelo**. No sabe que lo que le dije es mentira.
translation: Alberto **swallowed it hook, line, and sinker**. He doesn't know what I told him is a lie.

trato hecho *exp.* it's a deal • (lit.): deal done.
example: **Trato hecho**. Te compro la motocicleta.
translation: **It's a deal**. I'll buy your motorcycle.

uña y carne (ser como) *exp.* to be inseparable, to be hand in glove, to be as thick as thieves • (lit.): to be fingernail and flesh.
example: Oscar y Elena son **como uña y carne**.
translation: Oscar and Elena are **inseparable**.
SYNONYM: **como uña y mugre** *exp. (Mexico)* • (lit.): like a fingernail and its dirt.
ANTONYM: **llevarse como perro y gato** *exp.* to fight like cats and dogs • (lit.): to get along like dog and cat.

un hueso duro de roer (ser) *exp.* to be a tough nut to crack • (lit.): to be a hard bone to chew.
example: No pude convencer al jefe para que me diera un aumento. Es **un hueso duro de roer**.
translation: I couldn't convince the boss to give me a raise. He's **a tough nut to crack**.

vivir al día *exp.* to live day to day, to live from hand to mouth • (lit.): to live to the day.
example: Mucha gente en este país **vive al día**.
translation: Many people in this country **live day to day**.

volver loco/a a uno/a *exp.* to drive someone crazy • (lit.): to turn someone crazy.

example: ¡Me estás **volviendo loco**!

translation: You're **driving me crazy**!

y por si fuera poco *exp.* and if that wasn't enough, and to top it off • (lit.): and if that wasn't enough.

example: Hoy me robaron la cartera, **y por si fuera poco**, tenía mi cheque en ella.

translation: Today my wallet was stolen, **and to top it off**, I had my paycheck in it.

ORDER FORM

SLANGMAN PUBLISHING

12206 Hillslope Street
Studio City, CA 91604 • USA

INTERNATIONAL:
1-818-769-1914

TOLL FREE (US/Canada):
1-877-SLANGMAN
(1-877-752-6462)

Worldwide FAX:
1-413-647-1589

Get the latest news, preview chapters, and shop online at:

WWW.SLANGMAN.COM

SHIPPING

Domestic Orders

SURFACE MAIL
(delivery time 5-7 days).
Add $5 shipping/handling for the first item, $1 for each additional item.

RUSH SERVICE
Available at extra charge. Please telephone us for details.

International Orders

OVERSEAS SURFACE
(delivery time 6-8 weeks). Add $5 shipping/handling for the first item, $2 for each additional item. Note that shipping to some countries may be more expensive. Please contact us for details.

OVERSEAS AIRMAIL
Available at extra charge. Please phone for details.

PRODUCT		TYPE	PRICE	QTY	TOTAL
AMERICAN SLANG & IDIOMS					
STREET SPEAK 1: Complete Course in American Slang & Idioms		book	$18.95		
		cassette	$12.50		
STREET SPEAK 2: Complete Course in American Slang & Idioms		book	$21.95		
		cassette	$12.50		
STREET SPEAK 3: Complete Course in American Slang & Idioms		book	$21.95		
		cassette	$12.50		
SPANISH SLANG & IDIOMS					
STREET SPANISH 1: The Best of Spanish Slang		book	$16.95		
		cassette	$12.50		
STREET SPANISH 2: The Best of Spanish Idioms		book	$16.95		
		cassette	$12.50		
STREET SPANISH 3: The Best of Naughty Spanish		book	$16.95		
		cassette	$12.50		
STREET SPANISH DICTIONARY & THESAURUS		book	$16.95		
FRENCH SLANG & IDIOMS					
STREET FRENCH 1: The Best of French Slang		book	$16.95		
		cassette	$12.50		
STREET FRENCH 2: The Best of French Idioms		book	$16.95		
		cassette	$12.50		
STREET FRENCH 3: The Best of Naughty French		book	$16.95		
		cassette	$12.50		
STREET FRENCH DICTIONARY & THESAURUS		book	$16.95		
ITALIAN SLANG & IDIOMS					
STREET ITALIAN 1: The Best of Italian Slang		book	$16.95		
		cassette	$12.50		
STREET ITALIAN 2: The Best of Naughty Italian		book	$16.95		
		cassette	$12.50		
Total for Merchandise					
Sales Tax (California Residents Only add current sales tax %)					
Shipping (See Left)					
ORDER TOTAL					

prices subject to change

Name _____

(School/Company) _____

Street Address _____

City _____ State/Province _____ Postal Code _____

Country _____ Phone _____ Email _____

METHOD OF PAYMENT (CHECK ONE)

☐ Personal Check or Money Order *(Must be in U.S. funds and drawn on a U.S. bank.)*
☐ VISA   ☐ Master Card   ☐ Discover

Credit Card Number

Expiration Date

↑ **Signature** *(important!)*

ORDER FORM

SLANGMAN PUBLISHING

-PAGE 2-

See the latest products, preview chapters, and shop online at:

WWW.SLANGMAN.COM

QUANTITY	TITLE	PRICE	TOTAL
		Total for Merchandise	
		Sales Tax *(California Residents Only add applicable sales tax)*	
		Shipping *(see other side of form)*	
		ORDER TOTAL	

prices/availability subject to change

Name _____

(School/Company) _____

Street Address _____

City _____ State/Province _____ Postal Code _____

Country _____ Phone _____ Email _____

METHOD OF PAYMENT (CHECK ONE)

☐ Personal Check or Money Order *(Must be in U.S. funds and drawn on a U.S. bank.)*
☐ VISA   ☐ Master Card   ☐ Discover

Credit Card Number

Expiration Date

⬆ **Signature** *(important!)*